The Challenge Ahead

The Challenge Ahead
Information Technology in the Primary School Curriculum

Edited by
Joyce I. Fields
University of Hull, UK

ho **ap** **harwood academic publishers**
Switzerland • Australia • Belgium • France • Germany • Great Britain
India • Japan • Malaysia • Netherlands • Russia • Singapore • USA

Harwood Academic Publishers

Private Bag 8
Camberwell, Victoria 3124
Australia

3-14-9, Okubo
Shinjuku-ku, Tokyo 169
Japan

58, rue Lhomond
75005 Paris
France

Emmaplein 5
1075 AW Amsterdam
Netherlands

Glinkastrasse 13-15
O-1086 Berlin
Germany

820 Town Center Drive
Langhorne, Pennsylvania 19047
United States of America

Post Office Box 90
Reading, Berkshire RG1 8JL
Great Britain

Library of Congress Cataloging-in-Publication Data

The Challenge ahead: information technology in the primary school
    curriculum / edited by Joyce I. Fields.
        p.   cm.
    Includes index.
    ISBN 3-7186-5392-3.   — ISBN 3-7186-5393-1 (pbk.)
    1. Educational technology—Great Britain—Case studies.
    2. Computer-assisted instruction—Great Britain—Case studies.
    3. Education, Elementary—Great Britain—Case studies.   I. Fields,
Joyce I., 1943–
LB1028.3.C445   1993
371.3′ 078—dc20
                                                    93–20283
                                                    CIP

All royalties from this book will be sent to the Ainsty Churches Romania Orphanages Support Fund.

Thank you for your kind support.

Contents

Case Studies

Appendices

Preface

The information technology revolution has thrown up a multiplicity of challenges and opportunities for established teachers, newly qualified teachers and teachers in training. It has raised many issues regarding philosophy of education, pedagogy and classroom practice, because it potentially affects every area of the curriculum. Schools, like other large organisations, are not always adept at accepting and developing change. As primary-aged children have fewer technophobic responses than older children and certainly adults, it is crucial for trainee teachers to gain good information technology experience before they find themselves socialised into a school culture which is not favourably disposed towards information technology.

This book is not a "How to do it" manual, but attempts to raise issues and highlight challenges, and by giving illustrations from case study work from a range of backgrounds, to help its readers reach satisfactory conclusions. Also, with the advent of the new demands of the National Curriculum in England, there is a need to identify, through empirical analysis, the meta-cognitive development of young children's learning processes, which can be enhanced and attained earlier than is traditionally accepted, through the use of information technology.

As the technology document demands a new range of educational experiences the purpose of this book is to share with its readers the experiences of the contributors. It is hoped this will give rise to discussion and debate, which in turn may enrich the children's experiences throughout the primary school curriculum.

In chapter 1 an outline of the ways in which the role of information technology supports the "best practices of primary perspectives" is expounded. This is qualified with much reference to the legal requirements in various subject areas in the National Curriculum. The arguments uphold the main objective of all educators, which is to assist all children to fulfil their true potential by becoming independent thinkers and independent learners.

Stephen Heppell in chapter 2 highlights many real classroom problems, in particular the radical change in the role of the teacher which multi-media and information technology will inevitably make, the possible dangers of creating a two-dimensional world, and the dangers of moving too far away from pen and paper skills.

This is followed by a chapter on "The Release of Trapped Intelligence: Use of Technology with Communication Impaired Children" by David F. Sewell. The concept of normality of experience, the analogy of normal environment and the possibility of changing the environment to make it more accessible to the learner are all explored. It is also refreshing to be reminded that information technology is useful if it is appropriate to the task and more importantly, if it creates "want" in its user.

Peter Avis, Director of NCET, in chapter 4 examines the use of information technology as an appropriate tool, suggesting how to recognise what is the best form of utilisation, thereby avoiding using information technology as an end rather than as a means to an end.

In chapter 5, Michael Wright discusses the ways in which disability can be affected by the environment offered, and argues that disability should be catered for as a priority. It is essential that information technology is explored in terms of special educational needs whether they be in special schools or in mainstream schools. Whilst Michael Wright does not pretend to offer all the answers to special educational needs requirements this chapter should inspire its readers to ask the right questions.

As a practising headteacher, Derek Allen brings a healthy scepticism to chapter 6 and provides a welcome leavening to the complex question of utilising multi-media and micro-electronics in the primary curriculum. He expounds upon the impact information technology has had in some areas of the curriculum, while stressing the essential truth that no matter what its usefulness and fascination, it is no substitute for real life.

Chapter 7 deals with the experiences of one Local Education Authority in "the development of information technology capability" and "information technology to support teaching and learning" in a sensible and pragmatic manner. Readers will welcome the concepts of spectator, participator and creator and find good advice on the avoidance of making information technology areas too discrete.

The first of the case studies described in chapter 8 is a well-planned, well-executed ambitious task related to the dictates of a census. There is great precision evident in the work described by Michael Bortoft and the cross-curricular nature of the outcome is self evident. This is a very good working model which can be used in part or as a whole for replication.

Chapter 9 is a comprehensive illustration of how information technology can become part of the fabric of a major topic, and also, by implication, how the teacher needs a considerable facility with a wide range of software. Much stress is laid on the use of micro-electronic hardware other than the microcomputer, as well as the support and assistance from parents and other adults outside of the classroom. It will help perhaps to lessen the fears that some readers may have when faced with using camcorders, video machines, microcomputers, etc.

Rod Buckle in chapter 10 gives a thoughtful, sensitive and pleasurable account of the achievements of children whose horizons have been greatly widened through the use of music technology. I am sure readers will appreciate the scope of the achievement and how worthwhile this programme of study with these severe learning difficulties children has been.

It is refreshing to find real concern for equal opportunities, for citizenship, for economic awareness in "Movement: A Science Curriculum File Supported by Information Technology". This is a down-to-earth record from a very experienced teacher, which is most useful in that it addresses such topics as the differing expectations of boys and girls in areas of "technology". There is a common-sense approach to schemes, worksheets, availability of equipment and similar considerations for the practising teacher by a practising teacher, Alison Drage, in chapter 11.

The final chapter of this book is an attempt to gaze "Through the Looking Glass" into the twenty-first century and predict the ways in which information technology will support and direct future advances in the education theatre. It raises some of the issues which will have a distinct influence upon the evolution and development of information technology usage in the primary curriculum over the next decade. One of the most important is the European dimension as intercultural education heightens awareness of the nationalities and individual cultures of Europe, as well as their positions within the framework of the European Economic Community (EEC). Many classrooms throughout Europe are becoming multicultural in consistency, which was not the norm for school populations twenty to thirty years ago. This raises questions as to how well teachers are being prepared to meet these increased demands, and the effects of this intercultural fertilisation.

It is, therefore, no longer sufficient for teachers to be proficient in applying standard instructional methods and curricula appropriate for the majority of pupils to achieve. They must also demonstrate the expertise required to enhance equity and excellence for all in education. It is incumbent on leadership personnel and teachers to adapt proven methods to meet the goals of multinational and multicultural education. In my opinion utilising information technology will certainly go part way to meeting these objectives.

Chapter 1

The Role of Information Technology in Support of Primary Perspective

Joyce I. Fields

"The illiterate man of tomorrow will not be the man who cannot read, but the man who cannot learn."

[P. Williams, 1989]

The pupils of today are the citizens of the twenty-first century. They will be faced with a phenomenal increase in the ways in which information can and will be communicated, stored and retrieved. In 1979 4,000 new title books were published, this was more that doubled in 1990 when 10,000 new title books were published. So it is conceivable that over the next 8 years 25,000 new title books will be published along numerous other forms of information. Thus the skill of accessing and interpreting information from databases, spreadsheets and other electronic methods of storing information will be of paramount importance.

The main objective in primary perspectives, therefore, must be to enable and to ensure that such citizens become *independent thinkers* and *independent learners*. As information technology is a powerful tool for manipulating large quantities of data, literacy in this field will inevitably be one of the ways in which this can be achieved. However, one of the weaknesses of the ways in which micro-computers have developed in schools per se lies within the software market, which although through necessity has to be very competitive and offer a wide selection of options, has in fact had a confusing and very negative effect. Teachers and educators have found numerous difficulties because publishing software outlet have purported to fulfil specific aims and objectives to meet the needs of children and to fulfil the requirements of the National Curriculum. The reality has been that many 'hiccups' in such programs only come to light when being used in the classroom, which has caused frustration and disappointment.

With the national requirements changing in vocational, educational and economic awareness, Information Technology in the primary school curriculum must assume a role of major proportions. During the early formative years the foundations for a *'technologically literate citizen'* are laid and prepared, in order that an accurate ability to access, interpret information and draw sound conclusions can be developed. There is an urgent need for a clearly defined coherent policy of how, when and where these implementations and developments should take place as the potentiality of Information Technology presents the most significant challenge in the primary sector for both pupils and teachers in this decade.

As micro-computers in school can be viewed as a technology lead innovation they have been described as *'a solution looking for a problem.'* Unlike most inventions they did not develop because they were needed, they simply happened and their potential was initially recognized in industry and then transferred into the education theatre. The implication for the use of Information Technology in the primary sector was, therefore, wide ranging, covering issues in all elements of curricular, psychological, pedagogical and ultimately professional factors in primary perspectives.

In the education theatre micro-computers have enabled children to experiment with sophisticated ideas, allowing them to take intellectual risks which are not as easily made possible through traditional methods of teaching because of the volume of data becoming very clumsy and unwieldy to manipulate. Through their use children are able to discuss and reflect upon such ideas, thus presenting an opportunity for teachers to monitor the ways in which the children are tackling the problem at hand. It is very important that children are provided with opportunities to try out ideas and experience a variety of consequences, but it is of equal importance that any mistakes become an opportunity for experimentation rather than a negative experience of disappointment. Within this area, whenever children are dealing with numerical data they should be encouraged to develop an intuitive feel for how to interpret their data and to have a healthy scepticism for the reasons for its collections, processing and presentation.

Within the National Curriculum children are to be encouraged to
- communicate their ideas
- set and test hypotheses
- interrogate and look for patterns within the data.

Thus providing opportunities for various skills to be enhanced: *viz*
- systematical collection of data
- discussion and reflection of the use and nature of the data
- careful observation
- discerning similarities and differences
- methods of classification
- collaborative and co-operative interactions
- improve decision making to make balanced assertions
- logical organization of data
- encourage flexibility and creativity of thought

In the Programmes of Study and statements of attainment in Science attainment Target 1, Exploration of Science [level 1 to 3] and in certain attainment targets within Science Profile Component 2 [Knowledge and Understanding] *viz* The Variety of Living Things [NAT 2], Genetics and Evolution [AT4, NAT2] and Materials [AT6,, NAT4] children are readily involved in understanding of classification. Science level

4 requires children to *raise questions in a form that can be investigated, construct 'fair test', select appropriate measuring instruments, record results in tables and graphs and draw conclusions from the results.* Likewise in Geography level 4 children are required *to make various recordings of the weather and use a database to analyse and display the information.* Under the 'Historical Enquiry and Communication' History Programmes of Study for Key Stage 2 it is recommended that children *be given opportunities to analyse information in an Information Technology database and create graphs and pie charts to present information in the database.* The Programmes of Study in the 'Information Technology Capability' [AT5] of the Technology document suggests that children *should be taught how to store, select and analyse information using software, for example using a simple database package.* However, it is pointed out that children *should understand the need to question the accuracy of displayed information and that results produced by a computer may be affected by incorrect data entry* [level 4]. The above obviously suggesting a cross curricular approach with good inter-disciplinary management and organisation, but also serves to demonstrate that such experiences are no longer optional.

The Role of Information Technology in Primary Perspectives can be seen as supporting children in an active mode of learning:

> A requirement of all programmes of study is that pupils development Information Technology capability. Information Technology can help pupils investigate historical sources unavailable to them or difficult and time-consuming to analyse. Information Technology can help with historical enquiry and in communication the results of historical study ... History can contribute to Attainment Target 5 in Technology by developing pupils' ability in four of the five strands described in the NCC's non-statutory guide-lines for Technology'

> [DES, 1991]

Likewise, one of the main aims of primary perspectives is to assist all children to make sense of and understand their immediate world and their position and place within the wider world. The Association for History states :

> Computers do not make a historian ... One cannot see [however] how any future historian will be able to function efficiently without, at the very least, knowing how to find out if a computer might help and what to do if it would.
> [Arkell, 1989]

With the rapidly changing and moving developments in the micro-computer industry hardware has only a very short life expectancy, thus making the maintenance and replacement of micro-computers very expensive especially in the light of restricted Local Management of Schools budgets. As is very well documented in other sources, early educational software was very poor and short sighted *viz* drills and practise, or in a sense the principles of programmed learning were given a new lease of life. The new orthodoxy has moved to content free open-ended flexible programs, which can be adapted to meet the varying needs as teachers as educators have demanded much more versatile packages which permit an input to help the immediate learning processes, which are on-going in specific and /or particular classroom learning situations, which is one of the main objectives of primary perspectives and good primary practice. Thus resulting in a highly sophisticated and very professional approach to writing software to meet the needs of education as well as industry. Also, many of the good management strategies of industry have been transferred over to accommodate the demands and needed of schools.

Obviously, such effective implementation does not simply happen. It is the result of extensive pre-planning, thought, implementation, reflection, evaluation and appreciation and understanding of the 'hidden issues' taken place through the experience and expertise of teachers. The onus is always on the teacher at the coal face to make sense of the situation whereby micro-computers provide a new way for doing an old subject in support of the curriculum. Thus micro-computers are rightly used as 'tools' to enhance an already traditional activity, but with the added advantage of providing an empirical window into the mind of the pupils.

I would suggest that Information Technology in the primary curriculum, under the requirements of the National Curriculum, is best served through an integrated 'whole school' policy approach, which can be accessed through either thematic activities ranging and involving all subject areas, or through specific skills activities. A critical component of effective teaching is the assessment of the skills and understanding that children have and the follow-up of these evaluations with teaching to facilitate learning outcomes and the development of each individual. Thus a developmental perspective in early childhood education focuses on the developing child.

The essential element of utilising Information Technology should, therefore, be the provision of opportunities where children must learn to harness and take control for the appropriate use of the versatility of the micro-computer thereby acknowledging and recognising it as a very powerful tool within their learning experiences and situations. Good primary perspectives state that children should be permitted to develop their own personal strategies and powers to innovate, make decision and to create new learning situations. This can be achieved through the media of Information Technology resulting in children broadening their understanding of the relevance, appropriateness and usefulness of its power. Of equal importance is the need for teachers to have a clear vision of the potential and purposes inherent in Information Technology usage as each must go hand in hand if purposeful, effective results are to be achieved.

There is considerable potential for the psychological implications of the usage of Information Technology in the primary school. It is well documented that primary aged children engaged in the acquisition of skills and concepts, through the appropriate use of Information Technology and multi-media can be effectively enhanced and assisted as well as acquired at an earlier stage of development than is traditionally held. From the psychological and educational perspectives, the future of multi-media interaction within the primary school curriculum is proving very promising as it affords opportunities for children to produce their own ideas utilising an integration of text, graphics, sound, animation and video technology under micro-computer control. Whilst engaged in such complex tasks the learning processes which are evolving and on-going in the children's learning experiences are of the utmost importance. Therefore, the integration of discrete media types can effectively contribute to the learning processes addressing the individual needs of the users. HMI in *Information Technology and Special Educational Needs in Schools* advocate that Information Technology is making a unique and valuable contribution to the learning of pupils with special educational needs as well as children with special needs in mainstream schooling.

Likewise, Information Technology will make pedagogic demands but teachers and educators will not be faced with an 'either … or' issue of traditional teaching methods versus the integration of 'technology revolution' methods. By using the tool of Information Technology capability and its potential for supporting the identification and provision for purposeful opportunities for meaningful learning to develop it will be one of each style of teaching complementing and supporting the other. Both are invaluable resources for assisting children to create their own learning environments. Thus Information Technology teaching methods can be described as a mirror of the existing mode of teaching known as 'good sound primary practice'.

The professional demands which will confront teachers, educators, administrators, and those responsible for training services must be enormous for such a thorough going curricular input to be effective and to realise its full potential. The demands of the National Curriculum requirements, in my opinion, only go part way towards indicating the capability of Information Technology. Success will always rest with 'good' teachers responding to an innovation, absorbing it, finding out its positive attributes, and matching their classroom management, organisation and methods of teaching styles plus the learning styles of the children whom they are teaching with the facilities and opportunities on offer. Only experience and expertise can ultimately achieve this goal. Teachers are our greatest resource as they bring with them a wide range of talents and experiences. They serve as a 'facilitator of learning', a guide and a resource person rather than a dispenser of information and knowledge.

As a high degree of competence will be demanded from all primary teachers there will be a continual need for quality In-Service Training and up-dating for serving teachers plus a concomitant realisation of the legitimate needs for equipment and expertise in training institutions to establish the professional foundations from which newly trained teachers can develop their expertise and careers.

The aim of this book is therefore, to present a theoretical background to the ways in which Information Technology supports primary perspectives, while also providing working case studies for discussion and debate, through laying a sound foundation of varying challenges within this field. The role of Britain's membership in the European Economic Community is very important. Therefore it is discussed fully in the final chapter of this book 'Through the Looking Glass'.

The role of Information Technology in support of primary perspectives is, therefore, one of 'facilitating' through the means of a power tool. The twenty-first century will signal the change-over from traditional twentieth century *methods of teaching* to a technological concept of *learning*.

In conclusion, therefore, new uncharted waters are waiting to be explored. By harnessing their potential such learning can be incorporated into our understanding of the ways in which human beings learn per se. Exciting times are ahead, so teachers and pupils must have the courage to embrace and face the challenges which will empower them with the skills to be citizens of the twenty-first century.

> 'Individuals today have an increasing need to be able to find things out. Never before has so much information been available to so many, and never before have our lives depended so much on our ability to handle information successfully.'
>
> [Marland, 1981]

Bibliography:

Arkell, T. [1989] Analysing Victorian Census Data on Computer. *Teaching History* January: 18-25.

Cousins, P. [1990] Towards a Global Educational Database. *IT and Learning* 11, **4**: 90-92.

DES (1990) *'Information Technology and Special Educational Needs in Schools.'* HMSO.

Hemsley, K. [ed][1988] *Data Handling in Primary Science* Coventry: NCET

Marland, M. [1981] *Information Skills in the Secondary Curriculum.* Schools Council Curriculum Bulletin 9. Metheun Educational.

Williams, P. (1989) Director Computer Studies, University College of the North Riding, Scarborangh. (Statement made on a Course).

Chapter 2
Multimedia in the
Primary Learning Environment:
The Challenge Ahead
Stephen Heppell

Primary schools have barely begun the process of integrating the computer success-fully into the everyday processes of learning in the primary classroom. Before this challenge is fully met they are facing a significant leap forward in technology and the potential learning environment that it can resource. The challenge comes from multimedia—the powerful integration of text, graphics, sound, animation, and video under computer control.

An encouragingly clear international consensus amongst practitioners in educational computing has already emerged as to the (potential) general impact of information technology on the learner and on the role of the teacher[1]. As a taxonomy of educational application emerges, additional views may be observed, at the margins, built around specific categories of use. However, the consensus of general potentials is strong and finds clear expression through both the literature and through interview evidence. It is perhaps a measure of the task ahead that it is less in evidence through current curriculum and assessment outlines, or indeed through national development programmes at the in-service or pre-service level.

Briefly the consensus view of IT's impact on the learner may perhaps be categorised as:

- The child's relationship with knowledge becomes more participatory.
- The learning experience becomes markedly less linear.
- Learning outcomes are more liable to reflect student / institutional needs.
- The autonomy of small collaborative groups is enhanced.
- The physical limits of the learning situation are weakened.
- Vertical and horizontal continuity are engendered.

The consensus view of IT's impact on the role of the teacher may similarly be characterised as:

- A diminution of the role as custodian of knowledge.

---

[1] For example see the *'Information Technology in Teacher Education [ITTE]'* group's submission to UK Dept. of Education and Science Expert Working Group on Information Technology in Initial Teacher Education, 1989.

- A parallel growth in the role as counsellor, co-explorer, facilitator, knowledge guide.
- The greying of parameters of selection of learning groups (in age, experience, location and duration).
- The increasing complexity of the monitoring task in making formative judgments about complex process outcomes.

For the primary teacher, wrestling with eternal inadequate technological resources (although, one suspects, with generous provision on the horizon), this consensus is heartening, but the advances offered in support, as such radical changes to the teacher pupil relationship emerge, are minimal.

Into this already difficult arena emerges Multimedia. Multimedia delivers a technological imperative into our classrooms. We cannot ignore the learning environment that it offers, both because it will be delivering "edutainment" systems for the home (CDI players will be offering some form of interactive video to the home via "cheaper than video tape" recorders), and because the moving image that it presents, with rich aural and graphic presentations, forms a seductive and powerful delivery system.

At the "Information Technology in the Learning Environment" unit at the Anglia Higher Education College Multimedia tools are being developed for the primary classroom, appropriate staff development strategies, and the summative and formative advice frameworks that are needed alongside them. We are working particularly at repairing the fractured interface between primary and secondary phase education. For example, by giving primary children simple intuitive tools which allow them to author presentations of their text and graphics, mixed with others' video images, or high quality music sounds. We have been delighted (and not a little surprised) by the quality of work produced at this early exploratory stage and the opportunities it offers for progression. One simple current example allows children listening to Saint-Saëns Carnival of the Animals to explore the different instruments or animals by touching their graphic representation on screen. It also allows the option of listening, whilst drawing on-screen images that match the user's view of what the music tries to convey. In this example the music is from an audio CD, the images are previously scanned in from photographs and the text and drawings are the children's. We have sound sampled children's voices onto the software so that spoken cues are given by the children's peers. We are now linking in a video control option to allow children to act out the music through drama, video the result and drive that from on-screen, as the music plays. This is a very rich, exciting and complex environment for children to work within. It is indicative of the complexity which Multimedia offers.

Let us however consider some of the challenges posed by Multimedia environments:

- At the fundamental level of vocabulary, even with current technology, little progress has been made. Generic terms such as "Database"[2], or "Spreadsheet"[3] or "Networking"[4] can increasingly be found in the national education

---

[2]　UK National Curriculum Council Consultation Report 'Mathematics' December 1988 p58.

[3]　UK National Curriculum Council Consultation Report 'Mathematics' December 1988 p38.

[4]　California State Computer Education Coursework for the Clear Teaching Credential, July 1988, 80442, 3A.

documents of many Western countries. However, the language relied on to describe the processes expected to accompany even these common software applications in the classroom is (typically) seriously lacking. For example the teacher, observing children's word processed creative writing, finds language which is appropriate to pen technology (finished, original, best copy) inappropriate, yet no satisfactory alternatives exist (when is a story that exists on disc finished?). Multimedia also needs good descriptors although in practice everyday words like "Collection" or "Presentation" seem to do quite well.

- Similarly, whilst there are many competing models to describe children's understanding of, and interaction with, information these are typically two dimensional and are most applicable to simple learning environments (some children viewing environmental science through data capture into a spreadsheet for example). However Multimedia learning environments present the learner with a multifaceted array of information (and media) with which to interact. There are few good models to describe the interrelationship of understanding (or confusions) that may occur for the learner working with accessible sources including aura, visual and textual material in a technology rich learning environment[5]; the learner also faces the complexity of developing collaborative social and learning skills. Teachers and advisers wishing to construct appropriate tools for evaluation and comparison of pedagogic and organisational strategies need models of children's understanding.

Practitioners developing Multimedia tools are generally aware of the challenges that they offer[6], just as they are aware of the potential pedagogic revolution that they promise. This does not mean they have solutions to all the problems generated!

One final challenge centres on modes of assessment. Where a Multimedia learning environment functions as a central resource for individualised project based activity (serving as an information workstation for example, with an electronic encyclopaedia running on screen) traditional assessment focused on the individual is appropriate and manageable; the child's project is "product" and both formative and summative modes are applicable. However when the child works as part of a collaborative team generating largely process outcomes, and interaction is both with the information delivery systems and within that learning team, assessment becomes problematic. In the Saint-Saëns example above, how does the teacher allocate measures of attainment within a collaborative group who have been enjoying working with the music?

It would seem to be a good time to draw breath and wait for pedagogic developments to catch up with the hardware a little but again there are important, overreaching philosophical issues to be born borne in mind. Specifically, the children entering our primary schools today will be entering the world of work somewhere around 2008 ; this date is well into the "Information Age". If these children are to play their part in the New Age they will need not merely to be able to interact with and

5   Heppell and Owen. 1989 Workshop abstract for Computer Assisted Learning Symposium 1989, Surrey University: *'Lets have a Multimedia Experience'*.

6   Hooper, Khristina. 1987. Learning Tomorrow: *Multimedia in Education*, Apple Computer Spring 1987. "What happens when you combine the traditions of movie-making, workstation design, classroom teaching, library organisation, entertainment and psychology?

interrogate information, but to be able to be part of the whole process of data encryption, repurposing and capture. They need to begin to develop the problem solving strategies which enable this as soon as possible, and our teachers need to begin to use their good, tried and reliable education experience now, to maximise the opportunities thus made available. That is the challenge that multimedia presents, today.

Chapter 3

The Release of Trapped Intelligence: Use of Technology with Communication Impaired Children

David F. Sewell

Over the past decade, computers have become an integral component of many classroom environments throughout the world. In general, computers have been welcomed into classrooms as offering the potential for more active and varied involvement in the learning process, and providing the possibility for more effective teaching and learning. Central to such beliefs are that the cognitive development of children is facilitated when individuals are given the opportunity to explore their own thinking through interaction and communication with suitably designed learning environments. This, essentially, is a development of the view that humans are active, rather than passive, processors of information and that human cognition is more adequately explained by such a viewpoint.

The Enabling Technology

There are, however, individuals for whom active control and influence over the environment present considerable problems. Thus, a unifying feature of many handicapping conditions concerns the extent to which active control is restricted, both by the nature of the impairment and, in many cases, by the surrounding environment which may impose passivity on an individual. For such individuals, rather than being integral components or everyday life interaction and communication become sources of difficulty and anxiety—often things to avoid rather than seek out. Within this field it has become somewhat of a convention to regard modern technology, and particularly the microcomputer, as an 'enabling technology' in that it can reduce many of the demands and restrictions placed upon handicapped individuals, freeing them for other activities. Frequently, this 'enablement' is perceived in the context of the provision of improved prostheses—e.g. scanning devices, mobility aids, input devices, control switches—which make it possible for a disabled individual to interact more fully with the environment. Hawkridge, Vincent and Hales (1985) document many examples of technology being utilised in such a manner. The application of technology to act as an interface between the individual and the world has resulted in many dramatic examples which illustrate the potential of the technology to act in a liberating manner. In one of the most celebrated examples, Weir (1981) describes the case of an adolescent suffering from cerebral palsy involving all four limbs with an associated speech defect. The fact that cerebral palsy affects the output side of human performance means that conventional testing and assessment procedures are difficult to administer resulting in problems in the accurate evaluation of an individual's potential. In the case described by Weir, the provision of an appropriate performance environment (Logo with a simplified control system for use by the physically handicapped), resulted in the release of what Weir termed 'trapped intelligence'. In this case, a student who had presented major classroom management problems was able to demonstrate considerable academic potential as a result of technological intervention. Such was this student's potential that he eventually went on to be a successful university student. More recently, Weir (1987) has described in detail some of her work using Logo with children experiencing a range of disabling conditions. In a similar vein, Paul Goldenberg (1979,1984) has provided convincing evidence of the potential power of computer applications to enable children with special educational needs (autism, physical handicap, auditory impairments) to exhibit skills and abilities which had not been demonstrated under conventional classroom conditions. The success of such work illustrates the important distinction between performance and cognitive capacity, and that the former may be a poor guide to the latter. Although this has been raised in the context of the application of technology to special needs groups, it should be pointed out that the distinction was implied by researchers in the field of special education for many years (see Clarke and Hermelin, 1955, and Bortner and Birch, 1970), where the restructuring of tasks enabled mentally handicapped adults to display new skills revealing unsuspected abilities.

In such examples, the expression of hidden abilities was not consequent upon any change in the individual, but followed changes which made the environment more accessible to the individual. There are strong reasons to argue that an appropriate role for modern educational technology is to provide an extension of the learning environments available and accessible to the learner. This may be accomplished by improvements in technique or by the provision of suitable hardware of software—the principle is the same in each case.

The practical model of 'enabling technology' is thus one in which the environment is made more accessible to the learner, either by a restructuring of that environment, or by providing a means to allow the learner to interact more fully with the environment, or most effectively, by a combination of these two aspects. Technology, in many of its guises, is therefore placed in the role of being the interface between the user and the environment. In other words, technology is a means, and not an end in itself. If possesses the potential to act as a releaser for a range of cognitive skills as well as assisting in the development of new skills.

We should not, however, assume that simply providing access to technology via a suitable interface will invariable result in the development of enhanced skills. The application of technology should be guided by an educational philosophy which recognises the importance of communication and the role of computers as communication devices.

Significance of Communication

Learning of any kind involves communication between the learner and the surrounding environment. Within the cognitive approach, information is taken in via the sensory receptors (sight, sound, touch, smell), is transformed, given meaning and reacted to. Communication thus involves receiving, transforming and sending information in a process of interaction with the world. Thus,

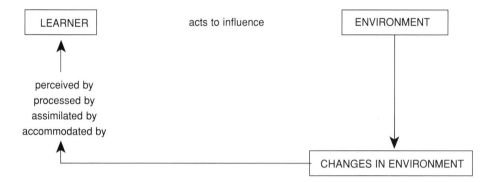

via this process the learner establishes mental models as a result of interactions involving both initiated actions and perceived, meaningful feedback. The schemata developed serve to direct future actions and to act as guidelines for behaviour.

Within this framework, communication plays a central role as it is via communication that learners influence the environment and also indicate the nature of their underlying mental models. Note that here, communication does not imply just speech—it implies all the means by which we interact with the world—facial expression, gesture, as well as vocal utterances, together with all our means of receiving information.

Effective communication thus requires reliable means of receiving input and making output. Clearly, children who experience difficulty in either reception or expression will also experience difficulty in communication. There is a unifying theme which links most areas of disability, which is that one consequence of disability is a reduction in both the quality and quantity of interaction available to the individual. Hawkridge *et al.* (1985) express it thus

> "For many disabled people, communication problems are the heart of their disablement and central to their personal struggle to learn to overcome their disabilities … They are often left isolated, powerless and dependent. They are deprived of important ways of expressing their individuality."

Consequences of Restricted Communication

Although the differing categories of handicap (motor, visual, auditory, speech, cognitive) show unique patterns of disability, often requiring specific forms of remedial treatment, underlying all categories is a restriction in the nature of interaction between the individual and the world. Most of us accept without question the fact that we can receive and transmit information about our thoughts, beliefs, abilities and emotions, and that we can experience the wide range of communicative sensations available to our intact senses. However, the situation is very different for those with a degree of impairment. Those who are speech impaired, visually impaired, suffer hearing problems or who have motor impairment all experience difficulties in communication, and the consequences of this restricted communication can be profound. Motor impaired children cannot explore their world and manipulate everyday objects with the same ease as can non-impaired children. They may be unable to reach and grasp objects, therefore finding it impossible to play with building bricks, jigsaws and construction sets. This lack of motor experience not only affects the quality of life experienced by such children, but may also adversely affect the development of certain cognitive skills involving spatial understanding.

Children who suffer early hearing impairment suffer from considerably more difficulties than simply enunciating words. Their whole auditory world is restricted and the consequences affect the entire structure of language perception and comprehension. Evidence from around the world on the linguistic development of hearing impaired children indicates that on average they lag several years behind their hearing counterparts in terms of linguistic skills.

A lack of interaction and communication with the environment means that a handicapped child is essentially deprived of environmental range and variation. The difficulties experienced in this respect by the sensory and motor handicapped are apparent. Less obviously, those with learning disabilities face similar problems in that they experience difficulties in processing and making sense of the range of information experienced.

Theoretical Considerations

Ulrich Neisser (1967) has argued that in a normal environment, objects and events possess implications for those in that environment. Neisser argues that individuals acquire knowledge and understanding from their interactions with their environments and that ultimately, experience and interaction are at the basis of the development of knowledge and understanding. Clearly, if one's degree of interaction with the environment is restricted then the acquisition of knowledge and understanding will be retarded.

Although Neisser's is a general statement, common to most models of cognitive development, it can be made more specific. Central to many theories of cognitive growth is the hypothesis that early motor experience is the foundation stone upon which intellectual development is build. Where motor problems exist, such theories predict that cognitive growth will be affected. A major influence in the development of such theories is Piaget whose theory suggests that a child's development of cognitive skills passes through a well-defined sequence of stages, with each stage indicating what the child can or cannot do. A cornerstone of the theory would appear to be that self-initiated actions and experiences form the basis of mental growth. As the child moves away from the dictates of immediate experience so progression to mental maturity occurs. Where self-initiated actions and experiences are lacking or limited, then that progression will be adversely affected. So, for example, the child is seen as first co-ordinating motor actions, then mental representations of these actions, and then sequences of mental operations. Thus, abstract knowledge appears to be traced directly back to physical action. Kephart (1971) writes:

> "Through these first motor explorations the child begins first to find out about himself, then the world around him, and his motor experimentation and his motor learning become the foundation stone upon which such knowledge is built."

A similar view is encompassed by Piaget's statement that "knowledge is derived from action" (1971). Within education, such statements as "children do not learn by sitting passively in their seats … "(Pulaski, 1971) and "the pre-school child … should be given tasks that allow him to act on objects" (Ault, 1977) can be seen as being in accordance with such a viewpoint. Clearly, within such a framework, children who experience a restricted degree of control over the environment seem destined to experience cognitive difficulties. Despite this apparently gloomy prognosis, there are well-documented instances of severely motor impaired individuals who are cognitively very able. The presence of such individuals must raise questions about the precise relationship of motor activity to cognitive growth.

In general, there is little direct evidence concerning the interaction of severity of motor impairment with cognitive expression. If the IQs of cerebral palsied individuals are taken as a guide, it is clear that, overall, this group scores lower than non-impaired individuals. Such evidence, however, does not necessarily support the view that motor impairment will invariably lead to cognitive impairment, since low IQs in cerebral palsied children may relate to the brain damage underlying the motor problem rather than to the motor problem itself. More significantly, Zeitschel (1979) has demonstrated that cerebral palsied individuals score lower on tests of visual perception when the test has a high motor component than when there is no motor component. Similar improvements in performance when the motor element is removed have been reported by Bortner and Birch (1962), suggesting that the problem lies in the motor act itself and not in the underlying cognition.

Meaning of 'Action'

Such examples lead one to conclude that the hypothesis that motor action is the foundation stone on which cognition is based is an oversimplification. Neisser's view is that our extraction of information from a situation depends on " … the individual's control of information pick-up." In Neisser's terms, interpretation of meaning (central to understanding) depends upon the activated schemata. For example, whether I process an individual's arm movement as simply "someone moving an arm", "someone greeting me" or "someone waving a fist at me" depends upon whether I expect to meet someone, whether I may have caused annoyance, etc. In other words, my interpretation depends on being able to extract meaning from a situation. This, in turn, depends on previously acquired and processed information.

Experience and interaction with the environment thus affect the development of schemata. Neisser refers to the development of schemata through "information pick up". Thus, individuals extract knowledge through acquiring information about situations. If the means by which information is acquired are disrupted, then, inevitably, the acquisition of knowledge will also be disrupted. One source of disruption is, as indicated, motor disruption. However, other disabling conditions also involve a disruption of the normal process of interaction. It can be argued that it is not motor movement per se that contributes to cognitive development, but that opportunity motor movement normally provides to link actions with consequences, to connect cause and effect, to develop schemata. Lack of interaction, not lack of movement, may more severely restrict cognitive growth. It may be that those severely motor impaired individuals who have developed good cognitive skills have achieved, in some way, a degree of consistent control over their environments via a modality other than motor movement.

Importance of Feedback

The basis of such control is the feedback the individual receives from the world concerning the consequences of 'actions' and future performances are modified on the basis of this feedback. If action/control is lacking, or if feedback is absent, restricted or distorted, then learning will be impaired. The interpretation of action is that it incorporates the notion of active involvement with the environment—i.e. if an individual is able to exercise some form of self-initiated control over the environment then cognitive potential may be optimised. A major problem experienced by the disabled is that such control and feedback are frequently distorted or absent. Thus, the motor handicapped lack motor control and motor feedback; the hearing-impaired are restricted in their linguistic control, and the learning impaired are limited in their ability to extract and process meanings and implications from the environment.

The significance of such control is emphasised by the psychological approaches of Bower (19979), Vygotsky (1962) and Bruner (1968). In the present context, the principle aim is to enable a disabled child to exercise control and to perceive the consequences of that control.

Effect of Restricted Communication on Personal Development

In addition to the more apparent adverse consequences of restricted communication upon a range of cognitive skills, limited communication also implies a restriction in social development. In many senses, human beings are social organisms. We rely on our families, friends and colleagues for a wide range of our everyday activities—simple conversations, jokes, shared interest, leisure pursuits. Most of these activities involve our ability to communicate. Restrictions in this ability will inevitably limit the range of social activities made possible.

The problem, however, extends beyond cognitive and social consequences. I recall being present in a classroom of hearing impaired children when they were required to carry out some work in written English. Their reaction was one of distress and lack of motivation and interest. They did not wish to read, nor did they wish to write. Contrast this with the same group of children several minutes later when asked to demonstrate on the blackboard how to work out some quite complex arithmetic tasks. A forest of hands shot into the air. There was enthusiasm and commitment, and a considerable degree of ability. Two commonplace classroom activities, presented to the same children within the space of 30 minutes. Both requiring the exercise of cognitive skills, both apparently equally difficult, yet drawing forth reactions of extreme contrast. Anxiety and avoidance for one task, enthusiasm and motivation for the other. Obviously, the English language task required the use of skills at which hearing impaired children are generally rather poor and *the children were aware of their problems with such tasks.* The arithmetic task does not involve linguistic skills, and so hearing impaired children have an opportunity to demonstrate what they can do, rather than what they cannot do. When I spoke to the teacher, her comment was "At English, they have a history of difficulty and of losing. At arithmetic they can be winners."

This statement contains very significant implications, as it relates to the way in which individuals evaluate their performance and their expectancies of future performance. A central aspect is that individuals possess, amongst other things, a set of cognitions about themselves, their abilities, their relationships and their interactions with the environment, and that these perceptions influence behaviour. Negative experiences and evaluations on a task can have deleterious effects on future motivation for carrying out that task. In essence, the argument is that a history of failure will adversely influence the perception of one's own abilities when faced with future challenges. Bandura (1977) has emphasised the importance of self-efficacy—the belief that one is able to control one's own life and deal with challenges. Within this is the idea that individuals with positive' self-efficacy possess self-confidence that they can deal with life's challenges. The other side of the coin is the notion of learned helplessness, in which there is an assumption within the individual that success is not possible. For such individuals, avoidance of challenge can become a way of life, with predictable consequences on cognition and emotional development.

Implications

These concepts have significant implications when placed within the context of handicap. As indicated above, a common theme in disability is that of restricted interactivity. This restricted interactivity also frequently involves a passive mode of existence rather than an active one. The nature of the disability may be such that passivity and dependence on others becomes incorporated into everyday life, and the child is able to exercise little direct control over the surrounding world. Within the cognitive model espoused here, this lack of self-initiated control has implications for cognitive growth. Moreover, within the framework of cognitive evaluation and expectancy, extreme passivity may result in a form of learned helplessness together with a pattern of low expectations. The low expectations may exist both within the individual and within those surrounding that person, with the inevitable result that he or she is rarely placed in a situation where personal control can be exercised in a manner that can lead to success and to positive self-image.

In discussing the use of computers with children, Papert (1980) draws a distinction between the computer programming the child, and the child programming the computer—between passive and active modes of control. In many senses, the situation is exaggerated for many disabled individuals. The nature of their disability is such that the environment controls them—this can become more pronounced when individuals are institutionalised. A common observation relates to the passivity experienced by many disabled children. An equally common comment is that we need to provide opportunities to break out of such passivity; that we need to shift the locus of control away from the environment and towards the individual. The advent of computer technology provides a means to achieve this goal. By the use of suitable interfaces, many disabled individuals can now exercise a degree of control which would otherwise have been impossible. The locus of control can be shifted, and the consequences for our understanding underlying capabilities may be profound.

We thus have a situation in which restrictions in communication have profound consequences upon an individual's ability to interact with the world, with consequences on cognitive, social and self development. A representation of this is shown below.

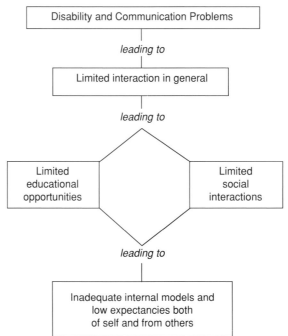

The history of our attitudes towards disability has included a concentration upon the nature of the difficulties experienced—i.e. upon what cannot be done. Although technology is not yet at a point where the disability itself can be treated, we can utilise the technology to offset some of the consequences. One major consequence has been a lack of interaction and communication—a restriction in the range of experiences that most people take for granted. We tend to overlook the significance of the everyday experiences of play and social communication, and in so doing we ignore their importance. To quote Goldenberg (1979):

> "It is so difficult to imagine not having had all the normal experiences—in fact, we are so totally unaware of them that it is difficult even to list them—that we may frequently interpret a handicapped child's failure to comprehend as a lack of intellectual capacity rather than a lack of information."

A major role for technology can be to act as a means to enable communicatively impaired children (and adults) to interact with the world in such a way so as to experience as wide a range of 'normal' experiences as possible. This is not an instance of seeking to 'normalise' the child but of trying to normalise the experiences. Central to cognitive and social growth are play, communication and challenge. For many handicapped children, such apparently 'normal' experiences have not been part of their life. We need to utilise the power and flexibility of the technology to make those things possible, and to provide environments in which cognitive and personal growth can take place, and in which autonomy can be developed. Simply providing suitable interfaces to enable communication to take place is a start, but, on its own, is not sufficient. It is also important to consider the nature of the environments and that of the interactions made possible.

The Nature of Computer-Based Environments for the Communicatively Impaired

The arguments presented above can be summarised by stating that restricted communication is seen as being at the heart of many disabilities. This restriction, involving limited interactions with the surrounding environment, has an impact of the development of an individual's internal models (schemata) which further reduces the interactions. This has consequences for the development of cognitive, social and personal skills. The implications of such an analysis for the design of computer-based intervention are clear. It is important to provide environments which enable an individual to break out of the cycle of restricted communication, which promote interactivity and which enable an active and positive role to be adopted by the individual.

Although modern technology can act as an enabling technology in the context of extending the range of experiences and interactions available to the disabled, this, in itself, is insufficient. If we consider how a non-impaired child comes to learn, it is apparent that much learning occurs in informal settings outside the confines of the classroom. An obvious example of this is the hearing child's acquisition of language.

A child's early years are filled with sound from parents, siblings, radio, TV, etc. Surrounded by language, most hearing children rapidly gain knowledge and mastery of conventional language. This enables them to ask questions, express opinions and wishes, and to discover more about their surroundings. In a sense, language is a biological enabling technology in that it makes possible many things which would otherwise be impossible. Perhaps less obviously, the everyday manipulation of objects gives a non-impaired child control over the immediate environment. From simple play activities come informal knowledge of spatial relationships and positional and relational concepts. In a more formal sense, what is argued here is that children build models of the world as result of their experiences with the world. Piaget has expressed this by viewing children as builders of their own intellectual structures. Children seem to be gifted learners, acquiring a vast quantity of knowledge before they go to school. As already indicated, if children are unable to experience the world, their intellectual development is likely to be restricted. To use the building analogy implied above, the environment, in all its aspects, provides the materials for building cognitive structures. If one is unable to access that environment, then the raw materials for growth will not be used. What is required in the context of communication impairment is not only a means to access these materials, but also to ensure that the appropriate materials are provided to enable intellectual development to occur. The pre-school non-handicapped child has easy access to such materials without our having to consciously structure the experiences, although we may seek to assist by providing educational toys, games and exercises. The handicapped, however, are not in such a privileged position. They are often deprived of both access to the environment and access to the materials which would assist their cognitive growth. Goldenberg argues that an appropriate role for modern technology is to help normalise the range of experiences available to handicapped children, not to normalise the child. The nature of handicap is such that even the most sophisticated technological intervention cannot fully equate the range of experiences available to a handicapped child with those experienced by the non-impaired. What is possible, however, is to provide the disabled child with environments which are analogies or 'models' of normal environments. Such environments can provide the disabled with access to important ideas more readily than a 'real' world equivalent. In other words we should seek to provide a range of experiences and opportunities from which knowledge and understanding can be extracted. Within this framework a child can operate on the environment and can perceive the consequences of those operations. This is what is meant by environmental interaction.

Sloman's (1978) view of the computer as a powerful educational toy is relevant in this context. Within the cognitive model of learning advocated here, we can see the significance of the word toy. In a sense 'toys' are needed: objects of learning which are motivating, which allow the user a degree of autonomy, which are personal and informal. The more that educationally significant concepts can be conveyed by such 'toys', the less restricted the environment will be. The notion of 'restricted world' has obvious relevance within special education because of the restrictions in communication. Technology can provide and otherwise perhaps unavailable opportunity for communication with a meaningful environment.

The Importance of Accessibility

The notion of interaction and schematic development implies that the nature of learning depends on both the learning environment and upon the present cognitive state of the learner, which defines the operations which can be carried out on the environment. More specifically, it depends upon the matching of the two. Designing learning materials implies not just a careful analysis of task structures but also a close attention to individual differences. What a learner gains from a situation depends on making a task appropriate to current schemata: information must be within reach (accessible to) of current mental models in order for that information to be processed efficiently. The learner must be able to carry out operations on the learning material, but at the same time the task should serve to display some of the weaknesses or limitations of the strategies the learner uses. All too frequently we underestimate what impaired individuals can do. In so doing, we do a disservice both to their self-esteem and to their potential cognitive growth. If we underestimate potential, we can be tempted to provide learning experiences which are too simple, which do not offer a cognitive challenge, which do not require the learner to 'struggle' to gain a deeper level of understanding, and which thereby fail to stimulate cognitive growth. This concept of 'cognitive struggle' is central to theories of cognitive development. Without it we fail to master our environments and develop our understanding. It is part of the model used here that struggle—not in the sense of encountering in surmountable difficulties, but in the sense of applying effort to understand a potentially significant environment—is essential for learning. As one parent of a learning-impaired adolescent said to me "I know he's not an intellectual giant, but he has the *right* to find things difficult so that he can find things out."

Accessibility thus implies more than simply providing direct physical access to, or control over, the immediate environment. As used here, it refers to cognitive accessibility, which implies providing environments which 'make sense'. Failure to make learning situations thus 'accessible' to the present cognitive state of learners has resulted in serious misconceptions about the potential abilities of individuals. Margaret Donaldson (1978) refers to a number of studies, dealing with Piagetian tasks, which suggest similar conclusions. The common theme of these studies is the need to construct activities which make sense to children—i.e. which are not alien to their experience, are related to knowledge of the world, and are in tune with their expectations and motivations.

Examples of Accessibility

Two related examples will illustrate the importance of providing activities which make 'human sense' to a child if we are to gain an insight into cognitive functioning and potential.

One of the dominant themes of modern developmental psychology has been that despite Piaget's major influence, his emphasis on what children could *not* do at certain stages of development resulted in an under-estimation of potential. A classic illustration of this is the 'three mountains' task. In this activity, the child sits at a table on which is placed a model of three mountains. The experimenter places a doll at various positions around the table, and the task for the child is : What can the doll see? The child may select on from a number of alternative pictures of the scene or may rearrange the model to represent the child's view. Piaget reported that there is a reliable tendency for children under 6 to choose a picture or model which represents what they can see and not what the doll can see, and this was taken as evidence for the children's inability to form a mental image of a view they could not actually see. However, there is good reason to believe that such a conclusion is premature. Martin Hughes (1975) carried out a similar task of 'egocentricity' but using a rather different task. The task was one which involved a social situation with everyday characters, but was one which could only be solved by perceiving a situation from another perspective. The cognitive requirements of the task were similar, yet Hughes obtained 90 per cent correct responses in a group of children aged between three and a half and five years. In a further study, Hughes utilised a simplified version of Piaget's mountains task, and by carefully structuring the presentation of the task was able to secure a high percentage of correct responses from pre-school children. It seems that the children in Piaget's experiments did not fail to reason; rather they failed to understand.

An example from Sylvia Weir's work (1987) also illustrate the point. She reports the case of a 13 year old quadriplegic who was presented with a version of Piaget's topographical task, conceptually similar to the three mountains task. In this task, the child and experimenter had identical models of the same scene. The task for the child was to place a doll in the same position as another doll on the experimenter's model. Weir reports that when both models were the same way round, the child experienced little difficulty. However, when the experimenter turned his model round, and then asked the child to place the doll in the same position, performance was poor. Superficially, this appears to illustrate the existence of an inability to handle spatial concepts. However, when the student worked on a screen representation of the experimenter's model performance improved dramatically. In this version, the student no longer had to place the doll physically. A screen representation could be moved by simple cursor control. When the task was carried out on the computer, the motor aspect of the activity was removed, and the student could concentrate on the essential cognitive requirements of the task and not on the problems of physically moving the doll.

Our understanding of the development of children's minds emphasises the importance of active interaction with the environment. This is something which many disabled children find difficult, but is also an aspect which technology has the potential to circumvent. The flexibility offered by modern technology makes it a perfect extension for a child who is not flexible. Through the appropriate application of technology we can provide the child with new opportunities for stimulation building on behaviours the child normally exhibits.

Goldenberg (1979) proposes that

> "......we can best serve the human being who comes to us for help by trying to remove barriers to his experiences, thus making room for him to develop his own adaptive and integrative abilities—room for him to develop autonomy."

Autonomy is often reduced for the disabled. Technology can act to serve as a means to provide opportunities to develop such autonomy.

Theory and Practice

Although such implications appear to be clear, transferring them into practice is less straightforward. The history of the relationship between theory and practice in education is one in which dogmatic assertions from the theoretician are greeted with understandable scepticism from the practitioner, who may have witnessed the rise and fall of several much-heralded educational innovations. Such a problem becomes particularly acute in situations where learners have a condition which impairs learning and where opportunity exists to structure learning by the use of powerful educational technologies. When considering the use of computer technology with the disabled both these conditions apply. The danger is one in which the application of the technology may result in a perpetuation of the passive mode of learning which may be present amongst many disabled children but which is at odds with our understanding of social, emotional and cognitive growth. Although a considerable amount of software has been produced for learning impaired children, inspection of much of this material reveals that it is dominated by drill and practice and rote learning, with the inevitable consequence that children are again placed in a passive role. Although drill approaches can play an important part in the development of automaticity, assisting in the rehearsal of lower level skills which will form the basis of higher order activities, it is a severely limited approach to adopt in the context of such a powerful and flexible educational tool as the computer. Programs written in what can be termed a drill vein tend to have three major flaws. First, they lack important interactive qualities and give little informative feedback, with the learner remaining quite passive. Second, they present a limited environment which allows few opportunities for the user to take the initiative and to take part in exploratory activities. Finally, and perhaps most significantly, since it encompasses both previous points, such materials are rarely designed according to the actual needs and abilities of users who, as people with communication disabilities, require structured situations where they can engage in meaningful interactions.

Such considerations have particular significance when placed in the context of special needs education. For example, children with learning difficulties commonly demonstrate low motivation and lack of attention on conventional classroom activities, especially when these are placed in an artificial or unfamiliar context which has no relevance to the child. This can be illustrated by a report of learning disabled children who could not carry out simple standard sequencing tasks, but who could recall, after several weeks, the sequence of operations necessary to switch on a computer, load the disc into the disc drive, load the program from disc and then carry out, from memory, the tasks required to play a computer game (personal communication from a Canadian teacher of the trainable mentally retarded). This latter 'task' contains the essential operations of a sequencing activity, but differs from traditional 'tests' in that the child carries out the operations in order to achieve a self-imposed, self-motivated goal and not one which is externally imposed.

In a similar vein, Weir reports the example of a 13 year old cerebral palsied girl who was apparently unable to use simple "forward", "right", "left" controls to manipulate the screen turtle to a target destination. However, when the task was embedded within another context, performance improved dramatically. In this case, the child selected cartoon characters from her favourite TV shows, and personalised the task by having the turtle visit the characters within her own story scenario. Several aspects are worthy of comment here. Again, we have an instance of performance being a poor guide to capacity. However, in this example, the provision of the initial computer-based activity does not result in the demonstration of 'trapped intelligence'. It is the modification of the task to make it fit in with the child's interests and motivations which result in the demonstration of improved performance. The task attained a personal salience in which she was able to draw on personal knowledge and abilities in order to succeed at an activity which had previously caused considerable difficulty.

Such examples confirm the double-edged nature of accessibility. The 'enabling technology' can provide direct physical access to otherwise inaccessible situations. However, equally significantly, it can help establish cognitive accessibility, via the application of appropriate educational techniques implemented using the technology. An appropriate role for modern technology is an extension of the learning environments available to the learner. Lumsdaine (1964) sees educational technology as being both:

a. Concerned with the use of equipment (as opposed to humans) in the teaching process (the hardware or product aspect of technology).

b. Concerned with the development of learning experiences, through the application of the sciences of learning (the software or "process" aspect of technology.

Application of Educational Technology

Educational technology thus consists of the appliance of scientific results and theories in the service of education. In special education, the use of structured training programmes, derived from psychological models, resulted in dramatic revisions in our estimates of the capabilities of severely learning impaired individuals (Clarke and Hermelin, 1955). In terms of the present schematic model of learning, a learning environment needs to be brought within range of an individual's schemata. Problems of motor, sensory or cognitive functioning possess a unity in that they imply a degraded quality of interaction with the environment. Changing the environment in order to make it more accessible to the learner will enable that learner to interact more fully.

Technology can act in a particularly powerful manner to become an 'enabling' device in this context. The work already referred to illustrates this process of enablement via technological intervention in action. What is involved here is the application of theories derived from mainstream psychology to the problems of communication impairment. The application of these models can have significant consequences across a wide range of disabling conditions. The work of Weir and Goldenberg illustrates how the appropriate use of technology to enhance communication and interaction resulted in reassessment of the capabilities of physically impaired children. The power of the approach is, however, not restricted to situations where there is a belief that intelligence is 'trapped', waiting to be released.

Our Children Can't Do That!

Rostron and Lovett (1981) report on the use of the interactive model with some of the most severely affected children. These children have been variously described in the literature as "crucial crib cases" (Killian, 1967) and "nonambulatory, profoundly mentally retarded, multiply handicapped" (Murphy and Doughty, 1977). Landesman-Dwyer (1974) lists seven defining characteristics of the group—extreme limited responsiveness to external stimulation; obvious severe muscular dysfunction; inability to move other than by simple turning; inability to attain or maintain a seated position; poor head control; abnormally small body size, and records indicating a "hopeless" prognosis for behavioural and physiological development, even with treatment. It is appropriate to consider the nature of Rostron and Lovett's work as it highlights how the model discussed here can be applied successfully to even the most severely impaired children.

Observations of children in the group leave a lasting impression. The nature of their disabilities is such that interaction with the environment becomes virtually impossible. There is an absence of motor control and movement, a lack of manipulation skills, lack of verbalisation and an extreme passivity. As Rostron and Lovett express it:

> "...as the children spend longer and longer in this state, the lack of responsiveness becomes self-perpetuating, preventing further development and learning."

The approach they adopted to offset this passivity was to develop very simple control devices which enabled the children to exercise some degree of control over the environment. Target behaviours (e.g. simple limb or head movement, pressure on a grip switch, blow-suck control) were reinforced using standard operant techniques with environmental responses including auditory, visual and movement rewards. The basic philosophy behind the approach adopted has been to provide aids which gave the children the potential actively to control and to interact with their surroundings and to extend the range of experiences available to them. The work carried out indicated that simple learning did take place in a group of children previously believed to be incapable of learning and of establishing cause-effect relationships. This work has been further developed by Andrew Rostron in the development of a computer-controlled 'buggy' for use with very severely motor and cognitively impaired children. This contains a variety of control options (simple switches, ultra-sonic beam, blow-suck control, pressure switches) which enable the individual to control the movement of the buggy—e.g. breaking an ultra-sonic beam with a simple motor movement results in the buggy moving forward for a pre-determined time. In this situation, the individual is in a position of active control—not the passive recipient of stimuli. By the judicious use of different controls, it is possible to built up a sequence of motor movements which can be used in other situations. Thus, for example, one child who used first the beam breaking option and then grip switch to control the buggy was subsequently observed to reach out for and grasp and object in front of her on a table. This was the first occasion on which such a behaviour had been seen. The degree of impairment experienced by these children is so extensive that such apparently simple actions have often been considered to be beyond them.

Phil Odor (1988) at the Communication Aids for Language and Learning Centre in Edinburgh has adapted and modified the approach used by Rostron in the development of a 'smart' wheel chair. Working mainly with cerebral palsied children—cognitively considerably more able than Rostron's group—the chair is designed to facilitate conscious choice and autonomy. The provision of simple control systems, similar to those developed by Rostron, enables the child to exercise such autonomy.

In both the above cases, technology is being used as a genuine enabling device, offering children the opportunity to carry out actions and behaviours they could otherwise not experience. Such devices are considerably more than mobility aids. They are aids to cognitive and social development, providing the users with the opportunity both to exhibit and to develop previously unexpressed skills. The approaches adopted by Rostron and by Odor share many similarities with the work of Paul Goldenberg and Sylvia Weir already referred to, with an emphasis on interactivity. Nor is this basic approach restricted to enhancing control for the physically impaired. Geoffrion and Goldenberg (1981) provide examples of communication with disabled children using interactive communication devices and stress the significance of providing interactive environments, and Ward (1989) documents the development of interactive language software for use with language impaired children.

The basis of Ward's work lies in the application of an interactive approach to language development influenced by the work of both Halliday (1975) and Bruner (1983). In Ward's 'natural language environments' communication-impaired pupils are able to enter a restricted, but purposeful, dialogue concerning a graphics environment presented on the screen. The language available enables them to manipulate screen objects, pose and respond to questions, provide descriptions and to give instructions. Although the language available is restricted, Ward's analyses indicate significant gains in language skills following experience on his computer-based activities. Work by other members of the Hull group (Sewell & Rotheray, 1987) has illustrated the application of this paradigm in developing software for severely learning impaired children. Using speech synthesis, together with screen graphics, Rotheray and Sewell have reported the development of a suite of software which enables severely learning impaired children to progress from simple cause-effect relationships to the exercise of problem solving activities requiring information handling abilities, memory skills and logical thinking. Guiding the development of this software was an approach which combined instructional design and cognitive learning theories, in which the requirements of specific tasks depended on the exercise of skills embodied within the software. The software was designed following a hierarchical task analysis which identified the essential pre-requisite cognitive skills at each level within the learning hierarchy. The 'target' end behaviour was for the learner to participate in a computer-mediated game involving multiple concepts, the use of question and answer skills and the application of simple memory and search activities. Children who initially experienced difficulty on single concept matching tasks (e.g. shape) were able to progress through the hierarchy to participate successfully in an activity which many of their teachers had judged to be beyond their capabilities. A distinguishing feature of this material, as within the software developed by Ward, is that its design principles derive directly from the application of cognitive and instructional theories to the cognitive and communication problems experienced by the intended users.

Conclusion

The purpose of this discussion is not to debate in detail the nature of the work referred to in the previous paragraphs. What characterises it is that it embodies an approach in which the implications of psychological models of learning are applied to the development of material for communication impaired children. There is an attempt to bridge the gap which often exists between psychological theory and educational practice.

The work reported here represents a view that providing enhanced opportunities for interaction not only influences quality of life and opportunities, but provides us with insights into hidden cognitive abilities. In this sense, the technology becomes a tool for both the learner and for the teacher or researcher. For the learner, technology can be a tool for communicating thoughts, ideas, opinions, skills, etc. For the teacher or the researcher the technology can become an evaluation tool revealing the presence of hidden or trapped potential. Use of the technology in the manner described here provides additional evidence that we are often guilty of underestimating potential. The use of technology to empower individuals to demonstrate skills which would otherwise remain unexpressed has a relevance which extends beyond the immediate context of its use with the communication impaired. It addresses the nature of cognition in a technological society. The work described in here can be placed in a context which again emphasises the importance of applying a psychological component to the use of technology with disadvantaged groups. Out of such application comes an appreciation that technology can be utilised to serve as an aid to cognitive expression and cognitive growth. As David Olson expressed it " … what the mind can do depends upon the devices provided by the culture." (Olson, 1976), but more significantly it depends on the intelligent use of those devices to serve as a means to achieve the goals of cognitive and personal growth.

References:

Ault, R.L. (1977) *Children's Cognitive Development: Piaget's Theory and the Process Approach*, New York: Oxford University Press.

Bandura, A. (1977) 'Self-Efficacy: Toward A Unifying Theory of Behavioral Change', *Psychological Review*, **84**, 191–215.

Bortner, M. and Birch, H.G. (1962) 'Perceptual Motor Dissociation in Cerebral Palsied Children', *Journal of Nervous and Mental Diseases*, **134**(2), 103–108.

Bortner, M. and Birch, H.G. (1970) 'Cognitive Capacity and Cognitive Performance', *American Journal of Mental Deficiency*, **74**, 735–744.

Bower, T.G.R. (1979) *Development in Infancy*, San Francisco: Freeman.

Bruner, J.S. (1968) *Toward a Theory of Instruction*, New York: Norton.

Bruner, J.S. (1983) *Child's Talk: Learning to Use Language*, Oxford: Oxford University Press.

Clarke, A.D.B. and Hermelin, H.F. (1955) 'Adult Imbeciles: Their Abilities and Trainability', *The Lancet*, **ii**, 337-339.

Donaldson, M. *Children's Minds*, London: Fontana.

Geoffrion, L.D. and Goldenberg, E.P. (1981) 'Computer-Based Exploratory Learning Systems for Communication-Handicapped Children', *Journal of Special Education*, **15**, 225-332.

Goldenberg, E.P. (1979) *Special Technology for Special Children*, Baltimore: University Park Press.

Goldenberg, E.P., Russell, S.J. and Carter, C.J. (1984) *Computers, Education and Special Needs*, Reading (Mass): Addison Wesley.

Halliday, M.A.K. (1975) *Learning How To Mean: Explorations in the Development of Language*, London: Edward Arnold.

Hawkridge, D., Vincent, T. and Hale, D. (1985) *New Information Technology in the Education of Disabled Children and Adults*, London: Croom Helm.

Hughes, M. *Egocentrism in Pre-School Children*, unpublished Doctoral dissertation, University of Edinburgh.

Lumsdaine, A.A. (1964) 'Educational Technology: Issues and Problems', in Lange, P.C. (ed) *Programmed Instruction: The Sixty Sixth Yearbook of the National Society for the Study of Education*, Chicago: NSSE.

Odor, J.P. (1988) 'Computer Toolkits in Special Education', in Collins, J.H., N. Estes and D. Walker (eds), *Proceedings of the Fifth International Conference on Technology and Education*, Edinburgh: CEP Consultants.

Kephart, N.C. (1971) *The Slow Learner in the Classroom*, Columbus: Merrill.

Killian, E.W. (1967), New Approaches to Teach Children, hitherto Crucial Crib Cases', unpublished paper presented at the *91st Meeting of the American Association of Mental Deficiency*.

Landesman-Dwyer, S. (1974) *A Description and Modification of the Behavior of Nonambulatory Profoundly Mentally Retarded Children*, unpublished Doctoral dissertation: University of Washington.

Olson, D.R. (1976) 'Culture, Technology and Intellect', in Resnick, L.B. (ed) *The Nature of Intelligence*, Hillsdale: Erlbaum.

Murphy, R.J. and Doughty, N.R. (1977) 'Establishment of Controlled Arm Movements in Profoundly Retarded Students using Response Contingent Vibratory Stimulation', *American Journal of Mental Deficiency*, **82**(2) 212-216.

Papert, S. (1980) *Mindstorms: Children, Computers and Powerful Ideas*, Brighton: Harvester.

Piaget, J. (1971) *Science of Education and the Psychology of the Child*, New York: Viking.

Pulaski, M.A.B. (1971) *Understanding Piaget*, New York: Harper and Row.

Rostron, A.B. and Lovett, S. (1981) 'A New Outlook With the Computer', Special Education: Forward Trends, **8**(4), 29-31.

Sewell, D.F. and Rotheray, D.R. (1987) 'Our Children Can't Do That! The Under-estimation of Ability: Implications for Software Design', *European Journal of Special Needs Education*, **2**(2), 103-110.

Sloman, A. (1982) *The Computer Revolution in Philosophy*, Brighton: Harvester.

Vygotsky, L.S. (1962) *Thought and Language*, Cambridge (Mass): MIT Press.

Ward, R.D. (1989) 'Some Uses of Natural Language Interfaces in Computer-Assisted Language Learning', Instructional Science, **18,** 45-61.

Weir, S. (1961) 'Logo and the Exceptional Child', *Microcomputing*, September, 76-83.

Weir, S. (1987) *Cultivating Minds: A Logo Casebook*, New York: Harper and Row.

Zeitschel, K.A., Kalish, R.A. and Colarrusso, R. (1979) 'Visual Perception Tests Used With Physically Handicapped Children', *Academic Therapies*, **14**, 565-576.

Chapter 4
Information Technology Capability and the Primary School
Peter Avis

The implementation and requirements of the National Curriculum are now established in most schools throughout England. Through the various subjects areas teachers are required to provide learning experiences which will enhance and help to develop information technology capability with all pupils.

What is 'Capability'?

It is interesting that the word 'capability' is used by the Statutory orders as the main thrust and emphasis in the Technology document is on pupils being actively involved in doing things! In the foreword of their report the National Curriculum Council state:

> Technology is the one subject in the National Curriculum that is directly concerned with generating ideas, making and doing. In emphasising the importance of practical capability, and providing opportunities for pupils to develop their powers to innovate, to make decisions, to create new solutions, it can play an unique role.

In brief the Technology document is divided into two distinct sections. Attainment Targets 1 – 4 create on profile component: *Design and Technology Capability*, and the fifth Attainment Target creates another profile component which is *Information Technology Capability*. This is the section which this chapter will attempt to deal with, as it raises various issues within the question why is information technology treated differently from the rest of the Technology document? In order to set the scene it is first of all necessary to give a clear statement of the terminology used within the Technology document.

Information Technology Capability

The definition of the attainment target for information technology capability is:

Pupils should be able to use information technology to:
> *communicate and handle information*
> *design, develop, explore and evaluate models of real or imaginary situations*
> *measure physical quantities and control movement*

They should be able to make informed judgements about the application and importance of information technology, and its effect on the quality of life.

These statements of capability are further split into different levels of attainment, whereby the attainment target means five different types of activity:

- *communicating information by computer*
- *handling information by computer*
- *creating and using models on computers*
- *controlling and measuring electrical signals by computers*
- *exploring the applications of Information Technology*

What Do These Mean?

Communicating information

The computer is an extremely useful tool for presenting and communicating information in a variety of flexible modes. It may be used as a word processor to type in text which can then be edited and reproduced using the desktop publishing facilities of the software package. Or used as an art package for creating an original piece of art or a poster, or as a music program for creating a piece of music, or as a database or spreadsheet. Its versatility can help pupils develop and present their ideas which can be made readily accessible and available to others.

Handling Information

The computer can effectively assist pupils in the way in which they collect, organise, store and access information. Databases and spreadsheets are often used for a variety of activities which involve the numerous skills needed when creating, storing, interrogating, calculating and presenting information. Stonier (1983) gives a precise clear definition of these skills when he states:

> ''Data' is a series of disconnected facts and observations. These may be converted to 'information' by analysing, cross-referring, selecting, sorting, summarising or in some other way organising the data. It takes work to convert data into information. Information is more valuable than data; it is data transformed into a meaningful guide for specific purposes. Patterns of information in turn can be worked up into a coherent body of 'knowledge'. Knowledge consists of an organised body of information, such information patterns forming the basis of insights and judgements.'

Hence databases and spreadsheets can be utilised in a wide variety of activities relevant to the National Curriculum in primary classrooms.

Modelling

The National Curriculum document uses the word modelling to refer to the way in which computers can simulate different situations easily, and can be used to create models of real and/or imaginary processes. These can vary from adventure games where an imaginary world can be explored; specific simulations such as trawler fishing in the North Seas, to a situation of an industrial chemical process which is too expensive or too dangerous to experience except through the media of the computer. All these activities involve the numerous desirable skills adherent within the primary classroom: developing problem solving skills, formulation of questions, testing, hypothesizing, collaborative discussions, re-editing, re-testing, etc. Hence giving pupils the opportunity to be more autonomous for their own learning. (Somekh and Davies, 1991).

Control and Measurement

It is intended for the computer to be utilised through the addition of 'buffer boxes' and/or special sensors related to specific computer software programs to assist young children to gain a clear understanding of their immediate environment and then the world at large. This is seen as being achieved through the sending and receiving of electrical signals which are inherent in activities such as making and developing a burglar alarm system for an area where the elderly live; controlling a railway crossing, etc. Young children should be placed in a situation of experiencing the trial and error strategies for working out the correct sequencing of events in order that a light sensitive sensor will trigger a series of electronically controlled outcomes.

Applications

Pupils need to understand firstly their own applications and the use of Information Technology. This may be achieved through the use of a variety of hi-tech toys prior to using the power of the computer itself along with its specialised peripherals such as the concept of keyboard. Throughout a young child's life he/she experiences the ways in which society has harnessed the power of information technology. Be it via the cash card till systems, supermarket check-outs, home video recorders and/or their use of the family's personal computer.

Progression

The National Curriculum (DES) (1990) states:

> Pupils' information handling activities range from early exercises in classifying
> and sorting familiar objects to structuring and creating their own databases ...
> Pupils develop skills in refining questions, identifying trends and patterns, and
> formulating hypotheses.

The need for the teaching of general information skills is of great import in the primary school curriculum, and this basic structure need not be altered with the introduction of the computer. It can indeed be greatly enhanced by permitting information to be handled much more quickly and also be presented much more effectively in a variety of ways which had not been possible prior to the introduction of the computer.

Primary teachers need, therefore, to provide numerous opportunities for pupils to cover the requirements of the level information technology capability. In order to assist in this and to demonstrate that there is a progression of increasing skills related to the different levels, the relevant attainment of targets have been divided into the five different kinds of activity listed above. Each of the following statements refer to paragraphs in the attainment target levels:

Communication

Level 1	–	Do they use computer?
Level 2	–	Do they communicate meaning?
Level 3	–	Do they create, then amend and then present their work?
Level 4	–	Do they save and then retrieve their work at a later date?
Level 5	–	Do they use different forms of information e.g. text and sounds, text and pictures for a specific purpose?

Organising Information

Level 2	–	Do they store and retrieve information?
Level 3	–	Do they collect, enter, retrieve information on a prepared database?
Level 4	–	Do they amend information on a database and check its plausibility?
Level 5	–	Do they crease the structure of the database as well?

Modelling

Level 4	–	Do they use a model and detect patterns on it?
Level 5	–	Do they form simple hypothesis about the model and test them?

Control and Measurement

Level 3	–	Do they give a sequence of instructions to control movement?
Level 4	–	Do they build a program to control movements of a robot or screen image?
Level 5	–	Do they understand a need for precision as well?

Applications

Level 1	–	Do they talk about ways equipment (toys etc.) respond to commands?
Level 3	–	Do they describe their own use of information technology?
Level 4	–	Do they review their own use of information technology and consider applications in real life?

Level 5   –   Do they know about personal information held on computers?

Each of these levels has deliberately been posed as a series of questions in order to allow the reader to make a clear decision as to what level the children are working at. This obviously, would be supported by the needs of the children to experience information technology in as wide and as varied situations as is practical and possible within the given classroom situation. For example, through topic based work the use of information technology should become an integral part of their learning experiences, *viz*

> *A walk around the local woods written up in the form of a class diary on a word processor – Communication level 3.*

> *Collect information about trees and enter into a prepared database – Organising Information level 3.*

Mixed Ability

Obviously children will have different information technology aptitudes and abilities, which may or may not correlate with their perceived abilities in traditional school subject areas such as mathematics, science etc. Tasks can easily be adapted to meet individual children's needs insofar as that a group of children can effectively work together to prepare and create their own database (level 5), whilst the teacher can prepare the structure of the database thus allowing children with less experience to enter data accordingly (level 3). The National Curriculum sees the school curriculum as a 'seed bed' or context (Birnbaum, 1990) for the development of information technology applications which has provided pupils with a very powerful tool for information collecting, retrieval and analysis.

Curriculum Analysis

Information Technology should fit naturally into the teaching styles and methods which schools utilised in their curriculum. It should compliment the on-going and evolutionary curriculum of the school and not overshadow the existing learning processes. A frequently used topic with infant aged children is 'Ourselves', a suggested analysis of the components of the National Curriculum subject areas being:

Mathematics
- measurements of body parts
- graphs
- area

Science
- body systems, blood
- structure, skeleton etc.
- senses

Art
- work inspired by senses
- texture and detail

Technology
- models of homes
- what makes a comfortable life

Language
- descriptive work around senses
- creative writing on feelings etc.

There is also a need to analyse each of these activities according to the aspects of Information Technology Capability. One of the first questions that needs to be addressed is: 'Can Information Technology enhance this activity?' If the answer is no then do not force the issue as it may well be that traditional paper and pencil methods are far more effective. If the answer is yes then identify the types of activities which are involved: Communication, Organising Information, Modelling, Control or Applications. Using the previous example of the topic 'Ourselves' this could be:

Communication
Using a wordprocessor encourage the children to write an identikit or passport description of themselves.

Handling Data
Setting up a database of the class with information such as name, height, weight, eye colour, nationality etc.

Modelling
Using a simulation exercise on keeping the immediate environment pollution free.

Control
Using a computer to create a simple system where lights in a model house are switched on when it gets dark or with the use of pressure sensitive pads when a burglar is present.

Applications
Looking at how Information Technology has changed the home environment and the ways in which video, satellite dishes etc. affect the occupants' lives.

Issues which schools need to address if Information Technology is to be effectively integrated into the current school curriculum.

Co-ordination
How, Why, Who and When? Development of a 'whole school' Information Technol-

ogy document? Who does the curriculum analysis? How, When and Where will all the elements of Information Technology be addressed?

Profiling

Staff and child development in Information Technology skills? Who will ensure the Information Technology element is for all children regardless of their aptitude or ability? What is the criteria for effective profiling?

Staff Training

Who needs it? What should it be? Who will execute it? How will records of achievement and staff development be maintained?

Assessment

Who is to be assessed—teacher, child, both? How is this to be done? Which are best ways of achieving this?

Special Educational Needs

Can Information Technology help? Do all children need special keyboards, extra support, etc.?

Equal Opportunities

How does the teacher organise the classroom management in order to ensure that all children have equal access? Is this really necessary?

Resources

Are they effectively utilised? Accessible? Security stored? Lists of hardware and software? Policy to meet their mismatch?

These are some of the issues that primary schools will need to explore to ensure that they are meeting the needs of the children to develop a sound progression of their Information Technology Capability.

Why is Information Technology Different?

As stated at the outset Information Technology has been split off from Technology as a whole. This has raised many questions as to why Information Technology is considered a different technology from the other technologies. Is this separation a result of its importance both as a tool for learning and its importance as a part of everyday life? Plus is there a danger that this will turn it into a separate subject within the curriculum, rather than being seen as being separately reported but taught across the curriculum?

Only time will tell. My stance is that Information Technology is special and is different from other technologies as it is the technology which children should use to learn and to learn to use appropriately at one and the same time:

> 'Individuals today have an increasing need to be able to find things out. Never before has so much information been available to so many, and never before have our lives depended so much on our ability to hand information successfully.'
>
> [Marland, 1981]

Further Reading:

Birnbaum, I. (1990) *IT in the National Curriculum—Some fundamental Issues.* RESOURCE.

DES (1990). *Information Technology and Special Educational Needs in School.* HMSO.

Marland, M. (1981). *Information Skills in the Secondary Curriculum.* School Council Curriculum Bulletin 9. Methuen Educational.

NCET (1990) *Information Skills and the National Curriculum: a Summary Sheet* NCET, University of Warwick Science Park, Coventry.

Somekh, B. and Davies, R. (1991) Winning the Class Struggle. *Times Educational Supplement,* 23 August.

Stonier, T. (1983). *The Wealth of Information.* Thames Methuen.

Chapter 5

Information Technology for Pupils with Special Educational Needs

Michael H. Wright

A future historian reflecting on the pace of change in special education, both theory and practice, over the past decade would no doubt perceive a changed legislative framework and a wide variety of practice emerging across the nation. Practices all of which aspire to move forward the philosophy underpinning the legislation through the development of a range of policies and strategies all of which are designed to change attitudes and practice in schools. With these changes we have also seen a decade of innovation and application of new technology in education, employment and the home, for people with disabilities and special educational needs. Perhaps it is in the application of information technology to the learning process which will be remembered as the coherent strand which links together so many of the emerging strategies—strategies designed to provide access to an increased range of social and educational experiences for all pupils.

The effects of the introduction of the National Curriculum for example on Special Education should be seen in the context of these changing attitudes and aspirations. The pace of change since the deliberations of the Warnock Report and its enabling legislation, the 1981 Education Act has been considerable. The concept of a continuum of learning experience along which all pupils travel at an appropriate pace sits comfortably with the Warnock view that "there are not two populations of pupils, the handicapped and the non-handicapped". However the implication that all pupils should follow the same curricular route brings with it a range of challenges for the profession. Mainly challenges relating to classroom organisation, differentiation and curricular access—more explicitly a needs led curriculum for all.

Handicapping conditions are an outcome of the social environment in which the pupil attempts to learn, it is the social environmental limitations which turn their varied disabilities into handicaps or alternatively provide for opportunity and success.

The concept of a needs—led curriculum is not necessarily integrationist, in the sense that all needs can not necessarily be met for all of the period of education within the same institution for all pupils. The social context of learning is important but not always achievable. The most effective use of resources has to be considered and hence for the foreseeable future some youngsters will continue to be provided for within special schools.

It should be noted that legislation and attitudes influencing parental and pupil entitlement has had the effect to date of increasing the range and level of disability seen amongst pupils with mainstream schools. This movement has also increased significantly with the increase in the range of technological devices able to support pupils in their learning.

Whilst no "discrete of different" curriculum is needed for pupils experiencing difficulty, modification to teaching and learning styles may be required. Many lessons can be learned from good special needs practice about classroom management, ordering the learning process, establishing match and differentiation observing and recording progress. There are also numerous examples of parental involvement and the pupil negotiated curriculum to be formed within the special educational sector of the service and also within good primary practice.

Pupils present a variety of characteristics which have to be addressed by their teachers. In many instances, it is becoming increasingly obvious to teachers in the special needs field that information technology provides a highly motivating pathway for pupils who previously found access to learning difficult. "NCC Circular 5" makes it clear that creative planning and teaching is to be required if all pupils are to engage in the full breadth of the National Curriculum. For many pupils if well delivered, this opportunity will bring enlightenment and breadth to a curriculum experience which has often been arid, narrow and basic skill orientated in the past.

This message is further amplified in NCC publication 2 "Curriculum for All"— destined to become the special needs reference document for the next few years. In this publication not only is curriculum breadth extolled but also the value of information technology as the major catalyst in bringing integrated curricular opportunities to a wide range of disabled or previously disadvantaged pupils.

I.T. is for the pupil what the mountaineer's ice axe and piton are to the climber; they are the devices which enable pupils to ascend to heights of achievement otherwise unattainable.

It would be inappropriate in an article such as this to attempt to list all of the various devices that have specific application to pupils with special needs. It is however perhaps worth considering some of the aspects of access which have been enhanced over the decade. There are numerous case studies to indicate the power of the various word processor packages which have led to the creative release of many pupils previously regarded as illiterate. Access to these programmes has only been possible for some pupils through parallel advances in speech synthesisers and the range of micro switch technology.

First hand experience in programming skills has become a reality for many youngsters through the development of a range of educational toys. *Big Track*, the *BBC buggy*, *Pod* and *Valiant* to indicate but a few.

Environmental control has become a reality for many pupils who previously experienced relatively low levels of stimulation whilst continually being totally dependent upon their carers to anticipate their every need. Their opportunities have increased in value and viability as switchgear has become more sensitive and computer systems more portable—the increased availability and flexibility of the lap top or wheelchair mounted systems offer obviously increased mobility and flexibility—when linked to a speech synthesiser the opportunities become endless.

Simulation programmes of all types offer a range of experiences to many non-ambulant pupils which would hitherto have been impossible—the "daily" increasing quality of graphics once more enhances the process.

The pace of development is exciting but particularly because for once the disabled are at the forefront of the process. The needs of individuals are seen as worthwhile challenges for many of the developers—mediphysics departments, computer scientists, programme writers.

There can not be an aspect of disability which has not been touched by these developments over the past decade. In most L.E.A's there is an increased awareness of the potential offered by I.T. and an increased range of both hard and software being made available to the pupils to support them directly.

Systems also are developed to support the pupils indirectly by monitoring their progress, by allowing them to interact with and negotiate their own curriculum pathways and also by assisting in the compilation of the total records of achievement.

How can information technology take a positive role in changing or helping change attitude and provide realistic, interactive learning opportunities for S.E.N. pupils? How can programmes be specific enough for individual learners needs and yet be marketable? Is any programmes use unambiguous and only able to match the particular pupil need at a point in time? Is it the programme or the mode of access which is important?

For some pupils, account must be taken of the 1981 Education Act assessment procedures next as it is only with this process that significant modifications or exemptions can be made to the National Curriculum and their individual access. This process has implications for all pupils who experience a learning difficulty at any stage. The Warnock Report suggested a five stage process; in Humberside this has been condensed to three stages, e.g.:

Stage 1   The work of the classroom—good teaching and a whole school response to S.E.N. enables the majority of learners to have their difficulties identified, assessed and overcome—usually in collaboration with their parents.

Stage 2   There are some pupils who require a higher level of intervention than is currently within the range of expertise of the school. Such pupils are additionally supported by a range of service staff who are routinely available to the school but who work peripatetically for the L.E.A. It is particularly within this stage that I.T. Advisory teachers play their part in the process, not only trailing materials but also extending the "needs" knowledge base thus informing the assessment process further. These strategies resolve the difficulties for many of the pupils but not all.

Stage 3   The small number of pupils whose needs cannot be met under stages 1 and 2 are directed to the L.E.A. for a full formal assessment under the 1981 Education Act. This assessment builds upon the information base collated under stages 1 and 2 and therefore should include an I.T. dimension. The process may lead to the production of a statement, a contract between the L.E.A. and the parents of a pupil. A contract which indicates the needs of the pupils—the resources needed to create an appropriate learning environment and a suggested location/school.

How often does I.T. feature in this aspect of the process? Perhaps this is an aspect of further development and growth.

When this is seen to happen opportunities for learning are extended through:

- improved levels of assessment
- oral interchange/interaction
- simulation and stimulation
- improved levels of motivation

We need a commitment and a significant change of attitude if the "Curriculum for All" is to become a reality, not just a document full of fine words and aspirations. For many of the pupils and parents we must be their advocates— if real opportunities are to emerge. Real opportunities for all really means quality for all and a significantly higher level of expectation for all. I. T. can provide the springboard for development and curriculum extension which is required - but only if it is fully integrated into the total learning experience of each individual pupil. When this happens it helps to provide differentiation and extension and avoids the "averaging" and reduced expectations levels which emerge in projects which identify categories of pupils and segregated or separate curriculum experiences. Care must be taken to ensure an appropriate match between pupil needs and precise hardware and software options. There must equally be a recognition of the need to resource and equip primary schools nationally in order that no pupil is disadvantaged or disenfranchised.

> "The experience of the last decade must provide the foundation for the next decade. Unless this is done, the potential for new technology will not be fully realised for those people with disabilities and Special Educational Needs."
>
> Dr. T. Vincent

Bibliography:

National Curriculum Council 'Circular No. 5', NCC, Alboin Walk, York.

National Curriculum Council, 'Curriculum for All', NCC, Albion Walk, York.

Vincent, T. 1989 [Ed.] 'New Technology, Disability and Special Educational Needs - some case studies'. [Distributed by 'Empathy' c/o Hereward College of Education, Bramston Crescent, Tile Hill Lane, Coventry. CV4 9SW.

Chapter 6
Information Technology and Childhood

Derek Allen

Think how different history may have been if Samuel Pepys had possessed a Psion Organiser. History consigned to a chip! Think how readable Chaucer would have been if he had been given a Spell Checker by the Wife of Bath. Imagine the twinkle in Beethoven's eye as he plugged his earphones into his Midi and synthesised into transferring his data into 'Junior Find' back on board the Beagle ... or the original Archimedes in his bath.

Would the 'greats' of history have written more meaningfully, composed more brilliantly, discovered, calculated, hypothesised, philosophised more deeply if they had had access to Information Technology? Most of them did not even have access to a pencil or a rubber. Just think what Da Vinci may have produced with Pro-Artisan or Caxton with a Desk Top publishing package.

The 'greats' are long dead, so we will never know for sure how their work would have been enhanced by Information Technology ... but we can conjecture. I would guess that it would have had no effect whatsoever. The hardware may have been of passing intellectual interest but would have quickly been discarded for the real tools of greatness; eyes, hands, feelings, balance, insight, inquisitiveness, passion, risk, etc. It was not the typewriter that wrote 'For Whom the Bell Tolls', but Hemingway. Not a machine, but a man drawing on his own experience of life and colouring them with a vivid imagination.

You could not escape the Black Death or Atilla the Hun. They existed. You could not ignore the flood if you were safe aboard the Ark ... you cannot dismiss the fact that the Earth is flat! All these were or are realities and will not go away. Neither will Information Technology. It is here to stay.

I remember our school cleaner's first reaction to a ZX81. She typed into it ...

"What is my name?"

The ZX81 replied:

"Sheila Garcia"[1]

Information Technology is not only here to stay but it is official and compulsory ... You WILL learn about it.

---

[1]   We had rigged it . . . she was impressed!

Science Attainment Target 1 Level 3:

- know that information can be stored using a range of everyday devices including the computer.

Science Attainment Target 1 level 2, 3, 4.

- be able to store information using devices . . .
- know that information can be stored . . .
- be able to retrieve and select text, number, sound . . .

Programme of study for Key Stage 1 (English):

"Pupils should be enabled to compose at greater length than they can manage to write down for themselves, by ... using a word processor. Pupils should be able to produce copies of work drafted on a computer, and encouraged to incorporate the print-out in other work, including displays."

In short you will learn about the whole spectrum of Information Technology from Sundials to digital watches and use computers to CONTROL.

> "All things bright and beautiful
> Computers great and small ...
> Make you wise and wonderful
> An Acorn makes them all."

But what is the expected outcome of all this, to use the popular new jargon? PAPER!

Consider: Ten Foundation subjects ... teachers required to update records at least once a year ... seven years in a Primary School ... 30 children in a class ... 1 sheet per subject ... 10 classes in the school ... Where do I put the 42 reams of paper records neatly held in ring binders? The answer is ... I do not ... I use Information Technology ... put it all on a disc.

"Disc error OC at Sector 1B":

My system gas failed the cyclic redundancy check and I did not keep a back up copy. Stop the disc drive ... I want to get off!

Now that cry may sound surprising from someone who spends most of his spare time writing computer programs and is currently writing a system that deserves at least a knighthood to help teachers cope with the planning and recording demanded by the National Curriculum. It is just that I believe that Information Technology is a waste of good computer, just like filling in a crossword is a waste of good pencil. You can do a lot with a pencil, not only can you chew it, you can write with it and draw with it. Shakespeare never had one, neither did Da Vinci, Einstein did but he worked it all out in his head. Just think what the 'greats' accomplished without even a pencil, never mind Information Technology.

So who invented Information Technology. INDUSTRY, and along with it was born the 'Trickle down theory of education'. Water down the business technology and let it trickle down into Secondary schools, water down again and let the trickle continue into Primaries ... and poor little Infants (Reception, Year 1 and 2) are condemned to data bases.

Information Technology is plagued with viruses, but it is almost a virus itself, pervading everything we do in schools.

It is as if the 'real' world outside, the adult world, wishes to supplant childhood. Business economics for 5 years olds … 'Identifying needs and opportunities', 'Generating a design proposal' … Information Technology is out of control. Not only does it dominate the world of works and increasingly leisure, but it is now insidiously invading childhood … and had their little eyes gleam. Intensely motivated by an insatiable desire to press buttons and hear beeps, quickly realising that the printer will save them the chore of writing, and they do not have to do it on their own … they can job share … children are quite happy to take Information Technology on board. At its simplest it can be a bit of light relief.

I try NOT to take a cynical view. Children do produce some impressive writing using computers in pairs—but they can produce equally impressive, if not more so, work in pencil on their own. How many great novels or plays were produced as a result of collaboration? *Macbeth* by Shakespeare and Hathway?

Writing depends at least on experience, on imagination, on love of language, an understanding of the human situation, its values and beliefs. My experience is different from yours, my understanding of society is different from yours … not better … just different! If we were to pool our understanding and experience we would not necessarily produce a deeper understanding or extended experience, but reduce all our values to commonalities and consensus, and our explanations and descriptions of experience become diluted.

If the computer has a place in the Primary classroom, and I believe it has, it does not depend on its role as a tool of Information Technology.

Science: Attainment Target 2: Level 2b.

"Pupils should understand how living things are looked after and be able to treat them with care and consideration."

The children will prod and poke the gerbils and the hamsters, weigh them, sort their food, draw graphs of tail length against time, all the things that children and teachers easily relate to. They will love their pets and they will learn much. But one day their pet will die! Then the children will learn much more. Some will experience momentary sadness, some will experience real grief. They will learn a little of how to cope with a real human situation.

When I wrote 'DUST' I wanted to see how the computer could contribute to the development of children's concepts of human experience. In DUST children are given the task of returning the ashes of a dead star to its resting place on Pluto. When the ashes are returned a new star will be born. Until then the forces of evil will rule. The children are told at the beginning of the story that the birth of the new star will bring HOPE. Little Bit was put in a cage on Mercury to demonstrate CAPTIVITY. Zia was also a captive on Venus. Through the children's efforts she gains her FREEDOM. On their journey through the Solar System the children meet situations which enable the consideration of … ISOLATION, WAR, TIME, PRAISE, JUSTICE, RULES, ORDERS, OLD AGE, RISK, PEACE. Little Bit and Big Norman, having vanquished all before them, realise that the only way to ignite the new star is to fly into the cloud of cold star dust and light it with a match. The cloud explodes and they die!

SACRIFICE … they return … RESURRECTION

It is a good program to present in the Easter Term. I have seen children cry when they realise that Little Bit and Big Norman are dead. I am not particularly proud of that, but it did demonstrate that a computer can evoke emotion, and that it could raise real opportunity for conceptual learning, as well as teaching the children a little bit of maths.

In DROOM you can find:

PUNISHMENT, LONELINESS, GREED, MODESTY, FEAR, MAGIC, DOMINA-TION, MISERY, FREEDOM.

In POND you can find SHARING, MOTHERHOOD, PREDICTION.

In WHISPY MOOD you can find ORDER, SURVIVAL, CO-OPERATION, PREDICTION.

Each program gives the teacher and child, in the safety of their classroom surroundings, the opportunity to consider the human situation. I hope that the children will never personally suffer loneliness, isolation, misery, punishment etc. ... but they do. Perhaps they may be helped to come to terms with these if we discuss them actively as opportunities arise in the classroom. But this is not Information Technology—no databases, word processors, spell checkers, psion organisers ... no Desk Top Publishing or Computer Assisted Learning packages ... no Deltronic buffer boxes, no Fischer Technic or Lego controlled models ... just good primary practice. Giving children experiences, helping them to develop conceptual frameworks, solving problems, having a bit of fun.

That is just what happened to Darwin. First-hand experiences, leading to conceptual frameworks, solving scientific problems, and I bet he had fun too even though his journals do not mention it.

Perhaps it is time to reverse matters ... to start to trickle upwards ... let us take experience into Secondary school ... (cannot afford the coach now that all parental contributions are voluntary) ... extend it into Industry and let them contribute to the improvement of the human situation rather than just profit.

Let us extend childhood and all its joys and frustrations, its irrationality and excitement. Let us not suppress it with Information Technology. For all Information Technology can do for a child is to help it become an adult too early. But it looks good ...

"We did it on a word-processor" says child.

"They did it on a word-processor" says the parent.

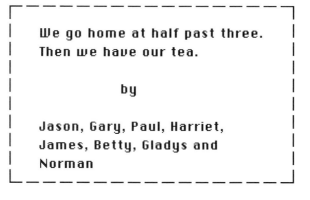

We go home at half past three.
Then we have our tea.

by

Jason, Gary, Paul, Harriet,
James, Betty, Gladys and
Norman

"I did it in pencil", says the child, "on my nown"[1]

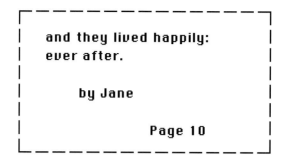

I have got three little mice in my computer … Albert, William and Prudence. Information Technology will do little to bring them to life, but imagination might. They live in Honeypot with Kenworthy the Baker, John and Elizabeth House, the Ladies with big hats who are quite important enough to be invited to the Mayor's tea party (really it is because they spend most of their time sitting on a seat outside the Dog and Duck), Betty Baily (an ageing Postmistress about to be replaced by Information Technology), and Andrew Smith a policeman with very sore feet. The problem with the mice is that they are blind!!!

Soon children will be able to write stories about them, preferably in pencil. I'll leave you to read their story and to ask yourself how it will develop children's thinking.

Down in the ditch hid three bandaged mice
Albert and William
And Prudence (who was nice)
She had muddy whiskers
Albert muddy knees
And shame upon poor William
He itched like mad with fleas.
They ran around his whiskers
And made his nose feel sneezy
He really was a sorry sight
And his little chest was wheezy.

---

[1]   This mis-spelling has been deliberately left in order to demonstrate authenticity.

Down in the ditch hid three bandaged mice
Albert and William
And Prudence (who was nice)
They really couldn't help it
You really shouldn't mind
The reason they were dirty was …
All three mice were BLIND.
They couldn't see the sunshine
They couldn't see the trees
But they sniffed the smell of cheddar
That floated on the breeze.

Up from the ditch came three bandaged mice
Albert and William
And Prudence (who was nice)
Their nose twitching madly
They bumbled through the flowers
In the shadows of their blindness
They seemed to run for hours.
Across the road they bravely charged
And up a path in their minds
As they stumbled headlong into church.

Down the aisle wobbled three bandaged mice
Albert and William
And Prudence (who was nice)
The cat crept from the organ
It was in hunting mood
It sniffed the air, and sniffed again
And sniffed some pussy food!
Mice! Its evil eyes went round
Mice! Its evil whiskers sighed
Mice! Its tummy rumbled loud
Mice! Its jaws were open wide.

Down to the altar went three bandaged mice
Albert and William
And Prudence (who was nice)
Ang! The cat crept through the pews
His tastes weren't very fussy
He didn't mind just what he ate
This death delivering pussy.
A gentle voice inside his head
Warned in words that were so kind
Do not eat them! Do not kill
These little mice are blind.

In front of the altar knelt three bandaged mice
Albert and William
And Prudence (who was nice)
They felt a touch of gentleness
They saw a blinding light
They rubbed their eyes with their dirty paws
And received the gift of sight.
Albert stood and stared around,
William blinked with eyes so wide
Prudence buried her nose in her fur
And just sat down and cried.

Up to the window looked three bandaged mice
Albert and William
And Prudence (who was nice)
They saw for the first time the colour of day
With the eyes of a new born child
Music echoed round the roof
And stained glass faces smiled
They threw their arms around each other
The cat began to purr
They danced in the light with the joy of sight
For a miracle had happened there.

Now near the church live three bandaged mice
Albert and William
And Prudence (who was nice)
In a little white-walled cottage
With a sometimes friendly cat
Where there's crumbs and cheese in plenty
Where mice can just grow fat.
Albert and William
And Prudence (who was nice)
And the story of the miracle
Of the three blind mice.

It is not Information Technology though, or is it?

Chapter 7

Information Technology in the Primary School Curriculum: The Humberside Response

Kathleen Guthrie

with contributions from William Hide, Rosemary Linsley, Anne-Marie Phillips, Richard Steel and Robert Rybak

Introduction

Information Technology (IT) has developed rapidly in Humberside when one considers that it is only ten years since the first DTI micro arrived in primary schools. A further boost to IT came in 1987 when each primary school was presented with a printer. Over the last few years there has been a gradual and fairly general move away from the drills and skills approach to the use of the computer through adventure/ thematic software and on towards the use of word processors, databases and other content-free programs. Many teachers are becoming less hampered by the technology, more confident in its use and more able to apply the uses to the curriculum. They are beginning to appreciate the notion of progression as being one of development within a piece of software throughout the school and of progression within the areas highlighted in the National Curriculum. Schools are aiming to harness the power of IT in order to help pupils gain access to the National Curriculum, increase their independence and develop their interests and abilities.

Although all primaries now have at least one computer, and many have more, until two/three years ago, most nursery teachers, and many infant teachers, had shunned the micro as being inappropriate for them and the children in their charge. Advances in suitable software for very young children have caused many teachers to look again at what IT has to offer. They are now using devices such as a concept keyboard to enable even the youngest pupils to engage in computer-linked activities.

The Place of IT in Schools

IT in schools may be considered in two main areas: *the development of IT capability* and *IT to support teaching and learning*. IT capability can be thought of in terms of content, where content encompasses skills and competencies. For example, the ability to use IT appropriately in suitable situations and to understand the range of IT applications and their effects on society. The second area, IT to support teaching and learning, focuses on methodology. The use of IT to support teaching and learning should contribute to and be enhanced by the development of IT capability.

IT Capability

The National Curriculum has highlighted five areas of curriculum content: **1.** developing ideas and communicating information, **2.** information handling, **3.** modelling, **4.** measurement and control, **5.** applications. Although it may be useful for teachers to give these areas individual status to clarify their nature, they do overlap and so should not be delivered as separate entities.

IT capability can be developed in these five areas. IT allows pupils to *communicate their ideas* in words, pictures and sounds to a wide audience. The use of IT in this area tends to encourage pupil creativity. When children are *handling large amounts of data* IT enhances the possibilities by allowing them to store, retrieve, alter and present their information in a variety of ways. It also allows them to establish relationships between elements of information and apply knowledge to tasks and problems. This area of IT use encourages pupil to apply knowledge. *Modelling* allows pupils to explore and experiment through simulation, to study changes and to make predictions regarding possible outcomes. Pupils can analyse and display data through the use of IT for *measurement and control* allowing trial and error. The fifth area of IT in the National Curriculum focuses on the *applications* and effects, causing children to consider the social, political, economic and moral implications of IT.

IT for Teaching and Learning

The use of IT *to support teaching and learning* has many benefits, of which these are probably the most important: it improves motivation; it offers curriculum access to pupils whose physical or sensory disability impedes their progress; it encourages iterative approaches to tasks and problems; it facilitates collaborative working; broadens learning styles; it helps to bridge the gap between abstract and concrete ideas and encourages a shift towards higher level competencies.

In the field of communication, a word processor allows the user to focus on the content, as the ease with which revisions can be made means that questions of spelling, grammatical construction and presentation can be left until drafting is complete, reinforcing the idea that writing is a process of refining rather than a once and for all product. Since mistakes are no longer permanent, they may be regarded as steps within the process.

Learning Styles

It has been suggested that there are three main styles of learning which pupils might experience. These may be thought of as "spectators", "participator" and "creator". All are important but there has, in the past, been a tendency towards an imbalance in favour of spectator activities. The introduction of computer-related activities helps to redress the imbalance by giving pupils more control over their own learning.

Special Educational Needs

The majority of pupils with SEN can participate in the National Curriculum and the task for schools is to provide a suitably differentiated curriculum in order to match the needs of the pupils and therefore to ensure success and access to the various statements of attainment. The school's scheme of work, perhaps through a topic approach, should take into account the need to break down tasks into smaller steps to enable access to that curriculum for those pupils who progress at a slower rate.

The use of IT can enhance the delivery of the curriculum for pupils with SEN as well as changing the emphasis towards the main focus of a given task, i.e. an appropriate overlay on a concept keyboard can assists a pupil to record the results of a scientific investigation. This would enable the pupil to participate fully in the identified task — learning about science. The five areas of IT capability mentioned earlier can be matched to individual needs in order to allow access to many of the statements which relate to IT. For example, the use of presets when creating a database can provide for a pupil who has learning difficulties the opportunity to be a full and active participant in achieving that statement of attainment (Mathematics Attainment Target 4: Handling data, Levels 1 & 2). Furthermore, an appropriate overlay on a concept keyboard can enable a pupil to produce structured sequences or produce an independent piece of writing using complete sentences (English Attainment Target 2 & 3 Writing).

For pupils with a more severe learning difficulty or physical disability IT can be an invaluable resource in terms of providing access to the curriculum. A range of IT related hardware, including a number of alternative input devices, is available to support pupils who are integrated into mainstream primary schools.

Support for IT in Humberside

The Humberside Microelectronics in Education Centre—HUMMEC—is a support centre for schools and teachers wishing to use IT to its best advantage across the curriculum. The Centre receives information from a wide range of sources. This information is then disseminated to schools via INSET, school visits, the Advisory Teachers and discussion with other interested parties. The Centre is actively involved in the evaluation of existing software, and in the development of appropriate software and related curriculum support materials.

HUMMEC supports and is supported by eleven Advisory Teachers, five of whom have a primary brief. The primary Advisory Teachers work in geographical regions and have experience of the entire primary and early secondary age range. Much of the team work undertaken by the eleven Advisory Teachers is cross phase resulting in a greater understanding of the whole curriculum. As a result of the developments outlined above the role of Advisory Teachers for IT is changing. Less and less are we being asked into a school to deal with a technical problem or to show teachers how to use a particular piece of software. More of the enquiries are curriculum-based which is partly due to the pressure created by the National Curriculum and partly due to a greater understanding of the role of the computer. In discussion with IT Co-ordinators, Advisory Teachers are able to help schools move towards formulating a school IT policy which can then be embedded within all subject areas and to develop an INSET plan for the staff which would be delivered/arranged in the main by the IT co-ordinator.

Much of the IT INSET work carried out in Humberside reflects the trend towards curriculum support. A result of the high demand on Advisory Teachers' time created by the implications of the National Curriculum is that we are having to look far more to support through INSET provision. This leads to teachers becoming more aware of the problems being experienced by others and that they are not alone. Because most courses are cross phase there is also a heightened awareness of the problems facing teachers from other phases, and a realization that there are many similarities between the phases. Although it can be expensive in terms of Advisory Teacher and supply teacher cost, work in individual schools are very effective in leading to real progress in IT across the curriculum. Flexibility of approach must, therefore be the key to Advisory Teachers' continuing support of schools as they develop their IT policies and integrate them fully across the curriculum. Thus facilitating the integration of IT into appropriate curriculum contexts, and thereby supporting the aim of all educators: assisting pupils to become independent learners.

Recommended Books:

Crompton, R. (1989) *Computers and the Primary Curriculum.* Falmer Press.

DES (1989) *Information Technology from 5 to 16. Curriculum Matters* 15, HMSO.

DES (1990) *Technology in the National Curriculum.* HMSO.

Phillips, M. (1990) For the record. *Educational Computing and Technology,* March.

Straker, A. (1989) *Children Using Computers.* Blackwell.

Case Studies

The following section in this book details specific case studies planned by practising teachers, which have been successfully executed with different ability children. The advantages of the following Case Studies are that the reader may use them as springboards to his/her own ideas or replicate and use the whole or part of the studies cited. Thus the reader may find that an extension of such ideas proported can enhance his/her own subject and teaching style.

Chapter 8

A School Census—A Computer-based Exercise in Data Collection and Analysis by Primary Children

Michael A. Bortoft

Introduction

This article is an account of a project undertaken with a class of Year 5 and Year 6 children. The aim was to use Information Technology to collect, analyse and order data to produce a report. It is not proposed as a model for other teachers to follow, but intended to illustrate the potential of IT as a tool for generating enthusiasm and communication skills in junior children.

A copy of the questionnaire and one group's section of the final report appears as an appendix to this article.

The Computer Programs

QUEST is an information storage and retrieval package or database produced by AUCBE

QKEY is a utility program supplied with QUEST which searches and counts keywords within specified fields of information stored on individual records. The program was modified slightly to reduce unnecessary parameters, produce a more attractive screen for primary children and a printout of results of searches.

BARS is a program that produces bar charts with up to 20 bars from information input by the user. This program was published in the magazine ACORN USER in 1985.

WORDWISE PLUS and INTERWORD are wordprocessors for the BBC micro produced on ROM by Computer Concepts.

SPELLMASTER is a spell check ROM also produced by Computer Concepts and used with INTERWORD in this case.

Computers are particularly good at rapid manipulation of large amounts of data, and this form of electronic record keeping is becoming an increasingly important part of the way we live. It is, therefore, vital that primary children are made aware of the advantages, and dangers, of information retrieval using microelectronics. Children should be encouraged to create their own data-files, and the fact that some of the files contain errors, and information that becomes rapidly out of date, should be used to point out the dangers of too great a reliance upon accuracy of electronic information. Gathering information about each other can also lead to opportunities for valuable discussion about other people's privacy and sensitivities.

[C. Schenk, November 1983]

Micros and Language in the Primary School

The Children

Class 2 at St. Martin's Scarborough are 32 mixed ability juniors, 14 of whom are Year 6 leavers and 18 are Year 5 children. The children already had experience of simple database use for keeping reading records, and the Year 6 children in the class had used the QUEST information retrieval package for compiling a database of Saxon place names the previous year.

The Stimulus

The idea of carrying out a census of school families was derived from the local pilot census taking place in certain wards in Scarborough in preparation for the 1991 national census. To publicise this event H.M. Census Office had invited local schools to participate in a census competition. The project provided a good opportunity for either introducing or developing the children's knowledge of the use of computers for handling and analysing large amounts of information.

STAGE 1 : The development and distribution of the questionnaire.

STAGE 2 : Entering the information onto the QUEST database.

STAGE 3 : Analysis of the information field by using an adapted version of QKEY, a utility program provided with the QUEST package.

STAGE 4 : The presentation of the analysis as bar charts using a graph program BARS from the magazine ACORN USER.

STAGE 5 : The compilation of a report on each field of information by combining the bar chart with a brief word processed report within a standard-ised page.

STAGE 6 : The final presentation by each group of all the statistics and analysis as a section of an overall class report.

Stage 1: The Development of a Questionnaire

The first lesson involved a discussion about the nature of a census with reference to the census carried out by Augustus Caesar, and a brief history of the census in Britain. Current census forms were deliberately withheld at this point to encourage the children to use their own ideas and not those derived from existing patterns.

Each member of the class was asked to write down a question they would like to see on a census questionnaire. These were then read out and a heading was written on the blackboard that each question might be classified under. From this activity there emerged 9 headings:

WHERE YOU LIVE	PETS
ABOUT YOUR HOUSE	HOLIDAYS
YOUR FAMILY	SPORT
HOUSEHOLD CONTENTS	HOBBIES
VEHICLES	

The children then organised themselves into groups of 3 of 4 and chose a heading which interested them. Absentees were co-opted into their friend's groups. The children were then told to discuss their chosen heading and compile a list of up to 10 questions for their own section. In this way we arrived at an overall questionnaire. Only then did we look at an original national census questionnaire.

This was useful as some groups had compiled questions aimed at families in general, while others referred to individual members of the family. By looking at the presentation of the national questionnaire it was possible to come up with a structure that suited each group. Because of the complexity of the final presentation it was decided that the teacher should word process the final document on INTERWORD to present to the class for final acceptance. The questionnaire (see Appendix) was distributed to parents. 188 copies were sent out from which 112 were eventually returned.

Stage 2: Entering the Information Onto Quest

As the questionnaire were returned they were organised into groups of 10 and kept in folders. Each questionnaire had been numbered and one taken home by the oldest or only child for each family in the school. As we did receive several expressions of concern regarding the use to which this information would be put. To protect the anonymity of families no request was made for names. This provided opportunity for a class discussion on the rights of individuals regarding information kept about them.

While the collection was taking place each group worked with teacher direction on compiling their own individual database of relevant fields on which to store the information. Discussion centred around possible abbreviations that could be entered into a field to speed up entering the information, and the fact that an empty field is in itself a response. Two weeks after the questionnaires had been sent out the children began to type in information. Four BBC computers were used on the project until the end of term when it was hoped to have all the information computerised by then.

Initial enthusiasm remained high with many children voluntarily giving up playtimes and lunch breaks to continue the mammoth task. The groups dealing with YOUR FAMILY, SPORT and HOBBIES had particularly large volumes of information to enter as their questions had been specific to individual members of the family. Group 3 dealing with YOUR FAMILY encountered difficulties as heights and weights were often entered in imperial units, and so they had to be provided with a conversion program to change measurements into metric units. Each record had a field titled ENTRY where the child entering the information inserted his initials as a record of work done.

The main problems with typing information in were due to small inconsistencies with spelling or spacing which may not appear to matter so much on screen yet were pulled out as different entries when analysed by the computer. The fact that a computer demands this degree of precision is of great value when educating children because they readily accept this imposed standard.

The majority of the groups completed the data inputs by Christmas and had some time to search through the records to correct typing errors. Searches were done through individual fields using QUEST query language to identify inconsistencies, and as some of the children rapidly became highly proficient at this task they were able to act as advisers to other groups with similar problems. As with many computer-based activities the development of language skills through co-operative discussion and problem solving was of great benefit to all. Children of all abilities had an effective role to play in the development of the project. As skills developed the teacher's role was subordinated to that of occasional adviser and arbiter of heated discussions.

Stage 3: Analysis of Information

At the beginning of the Spring term as soon as the student had settled into the class, the teacher could take each group with three computers in a library area for about three days each.

The first activity was to analyse the information in each field of the group's database. This was done using an adapted version of QKEY, a utility program provided with QUEST that picks out and adds the number of keywords in each field. For example in the field SEX that records the gender of each individual in the sample QKEY rapidly searches each record listed and provides the following data

238:M   222:F

The children soon saw the advantage of this method to doing it by hand especially as a printed version of the result provided a permanent record. The whole of the information on each database could be analysed in this way very quickly, and in some cases provided immediate results that could be graphed. In other cases, however, there was still too wide a range of results for effective graphing. In these cases further condensation of data had to take place through good old pencil and paper methods. In the case of HEIGHT, for example, the data was regrouped into 10 centimetre ranges from 61-70 cm to 191-200 cm.

Each child took the responsibility for a certain number of fields to organise the information for graphing. In delegating these responsibilities account was made of the ability of the individual. This was reflected in whether the children worked in pairs or individually. The ratio of one teacher to three or four children with three computers permanently on line made this task possible, and it would have been impossible under normal classroom practice.

Stage 4: Graphing the Data

Throughout the development of the project there had been several discussions on methods of presenting large volumes of data in an easy-to-assimilate manner. A decision about the use of bar charts for this purpose had been arrived at. The bar chart facility provided with QUEST is inadequate therefore the children were introduced to a graphing program provided through the computer magazine ACORN USER called BARS. This program is particularly good to use with junior aged children as they have direct control over the upper limit and number of divisions on the vertical axis. Also there are very useful facilities for providing text within all areas of the graph.

When the data was ready for graphing the children firstly created the vertical and horizontal axes by working out the upper limit of the vertical axis to the nearest 10, 20, 50 or 100 and then decided how many divisions were sensible. The horizontal axis was a matter of deciding how many bars were necessary to show the data. For example, only two are necessary for the field SEX as above.

The next step was to input the data for each bar which was drawn immediately after. The basic graph was then saved. The more detailed work now began with the labelling of the bars. This sometimes needed a key if there was insufficient space at the base of each bar for simple descriptions. Finally the horizontal axis was labelled and the whole graph given a title and the name of the person(s) who created it. When complete the graph was printed out, and each group discussed and interrogated what the graphs represented.

The complexity of the data provided a very good opportunity to extend the children's understanding of percentages. Using calculators they explored some of the more obvious statistics to present in their accompanying word processed report. This led to discussions about rounding off to the nearest whole number, and in some cases why the total of all the statistics did not make 100%.

Stage 5: The Word Processed Report

A brief report was compiled by members of each group giving additional information about the graph, usually in the form of percentages, and a simple description of any particular points the group wished to make. This was done on either INTERWORD or WORDWISE PLUS. Spelling was assisted on INTERWORD by the presence of a spell check chip. The whole process was useful to introduce how to construct a standardised page on a word processor without typing in the same headings each time.

Stage 6: The Final Presentation of Each Group's Section of the Report

At this stage each group put together their respective pieces of work into an organised section of the total report. This involved cut and paste techniques away from the computer to produce a single page summarising the data for one particular question, i.e. their word processed report with the relevant graph. Each section comprised of:

> A title page

> A screen dump of their VALUES screen from QUEST

> A printout of the QUEST data

> Printouts of the summaries from QKEY

> Pages of data summary and graphs relating to each question in their section of the questionnaire.

> A final page graphing the amount of data each child in the group had input onto QUEST.

Summary

This was a highly ambitious project and it was the enthusiasm of the children throughout the whole project that maintained the momentum. The speed with which they developed the computer skills and passed them on to one another was often surprising. The levels of discussion involved all abilities and, most important of all, each child in the class felt they had made relevant contributions to the final project report. Although this project was organised in a way that gave every child substantial periods of time at the keyboard, much of the individual progress was made away from the computer in organised or informal discussions. Many of the advantages of basic problem solving could be observed by 'listening in' to groups talking together trying to make sense of the data they had collected. The opportunity for a class teacher to spend prolonged periods of time with small groups from his/her own class is a rare one, and in this case the teacher was able to develop a greater understanding of individual children and encourage them to use developing skills in a practical situation.

Although it is not possible to undertake a project of this length and complexity without extra help it would be possible to take one or two sections of the original questionnaire as a class project to produce a less lengthy report, with children working in pairs responsible for making sense of the data from one question. Surely, it is much more meaningful to junior children to analyse data they have collected themselves through a questionnaire than to input facts direct from books, etc. The whole point of using a database is to interrogate data and come to presentable conclusions. If this data originates from the children's own enquiries then it has more relevance to them, and they have a feeling of ownership.

Bibliography:

Schenk, C. 1983 *Micros and Language in the Primary School,*

CENSUS

THE QUESTIONNAIRE

CENSUS TEST, SCARBOROUGH

Section 1 : WHERE YOU LIVE.

Please give the following information:

1) The town or village where you live:...

2) The parish in which you live:...

3) The Ward in which you live:...

****

Section 1 : ABOUT YOUR HOUSE:

1) How many people live in your house?...

2) Please tick your house type:

FLAT   TERRACED HOUSE   END OF TERRACE   SEMI-DETACHED

DETACHED   BUNGALOW   OTHER (please specify)...

3) How long have you lived in your house?...

4) How many rooms are there in your house? (Do not include separate

toilets, but do include bathrooms with toilets).

5) How many bedrooms does your house have?..

6) Have you got an airing cupboard?   YES / NO (please delete)

7) Do you have a garden?   YES / NO

8) How many doors are there in your house?..

9) What colour is the paintwork on the outside of your house?..................................

10) How many chimneys has your house got?...

Section 3: YOUR FAMILY

1) How many people in your family live in your house?..

2) How many children live in your house?..

Please answer the following questions for each person living in your house starting with the eldest as PERSON 1, and continuing in descending order of age as far as is necessary. If there are more than six persons involved please complete additional information on the reverse of this questionnaire. Please note that height and weight are asked for in metric measurements.

	1st Person	2nd Person	3rd Person	4th Person	5th Person	6th Person

----

AGE:

SEX:

HEIGHT (cm)

WEIGHT (kg)

SHOE SIZE:

COLOUR OF
EYES:

COLOUR OF
HAIR:

FAVOURITE
COLOUR:

OCCUPATION:

FULL TIME
   OR
PART TIME

Section 4: HOUSEHOLD CONTENTS

Please indicate how many of the following household items you have by placing the number after the item, e.g. if you have 3 televisions in your house you put a number 3 after TELEVISION:

TELEVISION 3

TELEVISION	VIDEO RECORDER	VIDEO CAMERA
COMPACT DISC PLAYER	HI-FI	RADIO
CASSETTE RECORDER	COMPUTER	WORD PROCESSOR
TELEPHONE	WASHING MACHINE	DISHWASHER
COOKER	FRIDGE	FREEZER
FRIDGE/FREEZER	MICROWAVE	TUMBLE DRYER
IRON	HAIR DRYER	FOOD MIXER
LIQUIDIZER	ELECTRIC KNIFE	

CENTRAL HEATING: (please tick)

GAS   ELECTRIC   SOLID FUEL   NONE

OTHER (please specify)..

****

Section 5: VEHICLES

If your family owns or has daily use of one or more cars please enter the details below:

MAKE	MODEL	ENGINE SIZE (cc)	COLOUR
1)			
2)			
3)			

if you own more than 3 cars enter additional details on reverse.

2) If you own one or more of the following vehicles please place the appropriate number after the vehicle''s name:

MOTOR CYCLES   BICYCLES   VANS   LORRIES   BOATS

3) Do you use the bus service:

NEVER   SOMETIMES   OFTEN

****

Section 6: PETS:

1) How many pets have you got altogether? (Please count tropical fish as 1 and cold water fish as 1).

....

2) Please indicate the number of pets against the names below:

DOGS   CATS   RABBITS   HAMSTERS   GERBILS

GUINEA PIGS   BUDGIES   HORSES   RATS

OTHERS (Please specify)...

....

3) Which is the family favourite?...

****

Section 7: HOLIDAYS:

The questions in this section refer to holidays taken during the current year, and may include holidays planned but not yet taken.

1) In a year how many holidays do you take that are for more than 2 nights away from home?

....

2) Please indicate where you took your main holiday this year:

ABROAD (please specify the country or countries you visited).

....

ENGLAND   SCOTLAND   WALES   NORTHERN IRELAND

3) If you took your main holiday abroad which type of transport do you prefer:

AEROPLANE   COACH   CAR   CRUISE LINER

OTHER (please specify)

                    ....

4) How many weeks a year does your family spend on holiday?

                    ....

✱✱

Section 8: SPORTS

Please answer the following questions in the same way as you answered questions in SECTION 3.

           1st Person   2nd Person   3rd Person   4th Person   5th Person   6th Person

----

1) If you play
sports which
do you like
best?
----

2) How many
times a week
do you play?
----

3) Which is
your favourite
spectator
sport?
----

4) How many
hours a week
do you watch
sport on TV?

Section 9: HOBBIES

Please answer the following questions as in the previous section:

	1st Person	2nd Person	3rd Person	4th Person	5th Person	6th Person

----

1) How many
hobbies do
you have?

----

2) Which is
your favourite
hobby?

----

3) How many
hours a week
do you spend
on hobbies.

----

4) Where do
you do your
hobby?

----

5) How did
you first find
out about
your hobby?

----

6) Does your
hobby need
special
equipment.

----

7) If so
please specify.

****

CENSUS

GROUP 1

WHERE YOU LIVE

by

Ginny

Victoria

and

Adele

VALUES   SPACE: **10968**

Infile   : **WHERE**   Max. Recs : **122**
Format   : **22**   Records :   **112**
Go   : **Max**   Fields :   **7**

Query :

Print :

Fieldnames :

     NUMBER   **CLASS**   **TOWN**

     PARISH   **WARD**

     EXTRA1   **ENTRY**

NUM	TOWN	PARISH	WARD	ENTRY
001	SCARBOROUGH	ST.MARYS	CASTLE	VH
002	SCARBOROUGH	ST.MARYS	CASTLE	VH
003	SCARBOROUGH	ST. LUKES	FALSGRAVE	VH
004	SCARBOROUGH	ST.MARTINS	WEAPONNESS	AB
006	SCALBY	SCALBY	SCALBY	VH
007	HUNMANBY		RYEDALE	VH
008	SCARBOROUGH	ST.COLUMBAS	NORTHSTEAD	AB
009	WEST AYTON	HUTTON BUSCEL	AYTON	VH
010	FOLKTON	ST. JOHN	RYEDALE	VH
011	SCARBOROUGH	ST MARTINS	WEAPONNESS	VS
016	FLIXTON	FOLKTON		VS
018	SCARBOROUGH		WOODLANDS	VS
019	SCARBOROUGH	ST MARTINS	WEAPONNESS	AB
021	SCARBOROUGH	ST SAVIOURS	FALSGRAVE	VS
023	SCARBOROUGH	NEWBY	NORTHSTEAD	VH
027	SCALBY	SCALBY	SCALBY	VS
030	WRENCH GREEN	HACKNESS		AB
033	SCARBOROUGH	EASTFIELD	EASTFIELD	AB
034	BURNISTON	CLOGHTON		AB
035	SCARBOROUGH	ST MARKS	NEWBY	VS
036	SCARBOROUGH	ST MARTINS	WEAPONNESS	VS
037	SCARBOROUGH	ST COLUMBUS	NORTHSTEAD	VS
038	SCARBOROUGH	NEWBY	NEWBY	AB
039	SCARBOROUGH	HOLY TRINITY	WEAPONNESS	VS
040	SCARBOROUGH	ST MARYS	WEAPONNESS	VS
041	SCARBOROUGH	NEWBY		VH
042	SCARBOROUGH	NEWBY	NORTHSTEAD	VH
043	SCARBOROUGH	ST MARTINS	EASTFIELD	VH
045	EAST AYTON	AYTON	DERWENT	VH
047	SCARBOROUGH	SCALBY	SCALBY	VH
048	SCARBOROUGH	ST LUKES	WOODLANDS	VH
049	SCARBOROUGH	ST MARYS		VH
050	CAYTON	CAYTON	CAYTON	VH
051	WEST AYTON	HUTTON BUSCEL	DERWENT	AB
052	SCARBOROUGH	ST LUKES	WOODLANDS	AB
053	SCARBOROUGH	ST MARTINS	WEAPONNESS	AB
054	SCARBOROUGH	ST MARYS	WEAPONNESS	VH
055	SCALBY	SCALBY	SCALBY	VH
056	SCARBOROUGH	ST MARYS	CASTLE	AB
057	CROSSGATES	SEAMER		VH
058	SCARBOROUGH	ST SAVIOURS	CENTRAL	VH
060	EAST AYTON	ST JOHN	AYTON	AB
061	WEST AYTON			VS
062	BURNISTON	CLOUGHTON	LINDHEAD	VS
063	SCARBOROUGH	ST JAMES	FALSGRAVE	VH
064	SCARBOROUGH	ST LUKES	FALSGRAVE	VH
066	SCARBOROUGH	SCALBY	NEWBY	VS
067	SCARBOROUGH	ST JAMES	FALSGRAVE	VH
068	SCARBOROUGH	ST SAVIOURS	FALSGRAVE	VH
070	SCARBOROUGH	SEAMER	SEAMER	VH
075	SCARBOROUGH	ST MARYS	CENTRAL	VS
081	SCALBY	SCALBY	SCALBY	AB
082	SCARBOROUGH	SCALBY		VH
085	SCARBOROUGH	ST MARYS	WEAPONNESS	AB
086	CAYTON	CAYTON	CAYTON	AB
087	FLIXTON	FOLKTON	HERTFORD	VS

091	EAST AYTON	AYTON	VH
094	SCARBOROUGH	ST MARTINS	WEAPONNESS	VH
096	SCARBOROUGH	ST LUKES	WOODLANDS	VH
097	BROMPTON	BROMPTON		VH
101	SCARBOROUGH	SCALBY	NBORTHSTEAD	VS
105	SAWDON	BROMPTON		VS
106	CAYTON	CAYTON	CAYTON	VS
107	SCARBOROUGH	ST JOSEPH	NEWBY	VH
109	SCARBOROUGH	ST MARTINS	WEAPONNESS	VS
112	SCARBOROUGH	ST MARTINS		AB
114	SCARBOROUGH	HOLY TRINITY	WEAPONNESS	AB
115	SCARBOROUGH	ST MARTINS	WEAPONNNES	AB
116	BROMPTON	BROMPTON	DERWENT	AB
117	SCARBOROUGH	ST MARTINS	WEAPONNESS	VS
118	SCARBOROUGH	EASTFIELD	EASTFIELD	AB
120	SCARBOROUGH	ST LUKES	WOODLANDS	AB
121	SCARBOROUGH	ST LUKES	WOODLANDS	AB
124	SCALBY	SCALBY		AB
126	SCARBOROUGH	ST LUKES	WOODLANDS	AB
128	SCARBOROUGH	ST JAMES	FALSGRAVE	AB
129	SCARBOROUGH	SCALBY	NORTHSTEAD	AB
130	SCARBOROUGH	ST SAVIOURS	FALSGRAVE	AB
135	SCARBOROUGH			VS
137	SCARBOROUGH	ST SAVIOURS	WOODLANDS	VS
138	BROMPTON	ALL SAINTS	AYTON	VH
139	BROMPTON	BROMPTON	DERWENT	VH
140	SCARBOROUGH	ST MARTINS	WEAPONNESS	VH
142	CROSSGATES	SEAMER	SEAMER	AB
145	SCARBOROUGH	ST SAVIOURS		AB
147	SCARBOROUGH			AB
148	FILEY	ST OSWALDS	RYEDALE	AB
150	HUNMANBY	HUNMANBY	HERTFORD	AB
151	SCARBOROUGH	ST MARTINS	EASTFIELD	VS
152	SCARBOROUGH		NORTHSTEAD	VS
153	SCARBOROUGH		EASTFIELD	VS
154	SCARBOROUGH	ST LUKES	WOODLANDS	VS
156	MUSTON	MUSTON	RYEDALE	VS
159	SCARBOROUGH	ST LUKES		VS
161	SCARBOROUGH	ST MARTINS	WEAPONNESS	VH
162	SCARBOROUGH	ST MARTINS	WEAPONNESS	VH
163	SCARBOROUGH	ST COLUMBAS	NORTHSTEAD	VS
165	SCARBOROUGH	SCALBY	NEWBY	VS
167	BURNISTON	CLOUGHTON	LINDHEAD	VS
170	SCARBOROUGH	ST SAVIOURS	CENTRAL	VS
171	HUNMANBY	HUNMANBY	HERTFORD	VH
172	SCARBOROUGH	SCALBY	NEWBY	AB
173	SCARBOROUGH	ST MARTINS	EASTFIELD	AB
174	BURNISTON	CLOUGHTON	LINDHEAD	VH
175	SCARBOROUGH	ST LUKES	WOODLANDS	VH
176	SCALBY	SCALBY	SCALBY	AB
177	SCARBOROUGH	ST LUKES	WOODLANDS	AB
179	SCARBOROUGH	ST MARYS	CASTLE	AB
180	SCARBOROUGH	ST LUKES	WOODLANDS	VH
182	CROSSGATES	SEAMER		AB
183	SCALBY	SCALBY	SCALBY	VH
184	SCARBOROUGH	ST MARTINS	WEAPONNESS	AB

QKEY   FINDS KEYWORDS. QUESTD & QUEST (V.2.3)
===

FILENAME: WHERE17   FIELD: 3 – TOWN

```
1    :    MUSTON
4    :    BROMPTON
4    :    BURNISTON
3    :    CAYTON
3    :    CROSSGATES
1    :    SAWDON
75   :    SCARBOROUGH
7    :    SCALBY
3    :    EAST AYTON
1    :    FILEY
2    :    FLIXTON
1    :    FOLKTON
3    :    WEST AYTON
1    :    WRENCH GREEN
3    :    HUNMANBY
```

```
QKEY                    FINDS KEYWORDS.   QUESTD & QUEST (V.2.3)
===

FILENAME: WHERE18           FIELD: 4 – PARISH

1    :     MUSTON
4    :     NEWBY
1    :     ALL SAINTS
2    :     AYTON
4    :     BROMPTON
3    :     CAYTON
4    :     CLOUGHTON
14   :     SCALBY
4    :     SEAMER
9    :     ST MARYS
17   :     ST MARTINS
7    :     ST SAVIOURS
13   :      ST LUKES
2    :     ST JOHN
3    :     ST JAMES
1    :     ST MARKS
1    :     ST JOSEPH
3    :     ST COLUMBAS
1    :     ST OSWALDS
2    :     EASTFIELD
2    :     FOLKTON
1    :     HACKNESS
2    :     HOLY TRINITY
2    :     HUTTON BUSCEL
2    :     HUNMANBY
```

QKEY   FINDS KEYWORDS. QUESTD & QUEST (V.2.3)
===

FILENAME: WHERE18   FIELD 5 – WARD

3	:	LINDHEAD
6	:	NEWBY
8	:	NORTHSTEAD
3	:	AYTON
4	:	CASTLE
3	:	CAYTON
3	:	CENTRAL
4	:	RYEDALE
7	:	SCALBY
4	:	DERWENT
2	:	SEAMER
6	:	EASTFIELD
8	:	FALSGRAVE
3	:	HERTFORD
18	:	WEAPONNESS
12	:	WOODLANDS

QKEY   FINDS KEYWORDS. QUESTD & QUEST (V.2.3)
===

FILENAME: WHERE18   FIELD: 7 – ENTRY

37   :   AB
3   :   AB
42   :   VH
30   :   VS

CENSUS - SCARBOROUGH

SECTION 1 : WHERE YOU LIVE

GROUP MEMBERS: Virgina, Adele and Victoria

QUESTION 1: Please give the Parish where you live.

When we did the bar chart fro the parishes we found out that from the 112 families who sent their census forms back that only 105 had been put in. 94% wrote the parish in the census and seven did not. On the bar chart we did St. Martins parish had the most with 17. We were surprised to see that Scalby was second with 14 because Scalby is out of Scarborough.

We did not put in all the parishes because the graph program only would let use go up to 20 bars. The following parishes had only one child going to St Martins school:

Muston, All Saints, St. Marks, St. Joseph, St. Oswalds and Hackness.

by Adele.

SECTION 1:   WHERE YOU LIVE

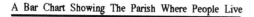

A Bar Chart Showing The Parish Where People Live

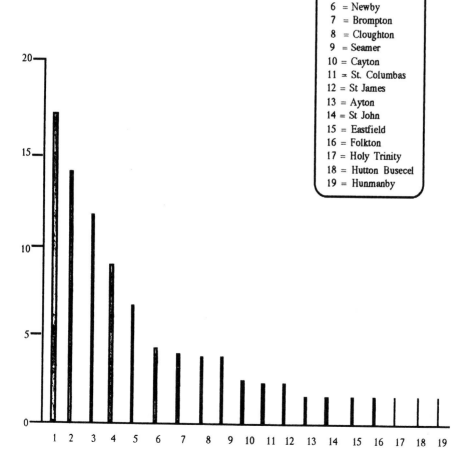

1	=	St Martins
2	=	Scalby
3	=	St. Lukes
4	=	St. Marys
5	=	St. Saviours
6	=	Newby
7	=	Brompton
8	=	Cloughton
9	=	Seamer
10	=	Cayton
11	=	St. Columbas
12	=	St James
13	=	Ayton
14	=	St John
15	=	Eastfield
16	=	Folkton
17	=	Holy Trinity
18	=	Hutton Busecel
19	=	Hunmanby

CENSUS - SCARBOROUGH

SECTION 1 : WHERE YOU LIVE

GROUP MEMBERS: Virgina, Adele and Victoria

Question 1: Please give the Town or Village where you live.

We found out when we did the chart that most people who went to our school are living in Scarbrough town. 75 people were living in Scarborough.

Our school is a Church of England school so people from the Deanery of Scarbrough can send their children to St. Martins. This explains why we have some families who do not live in Scarborough.

67% of the families who returned the census lived in Scarborough.

by Adele

SECTION 1 : WHERE YOU LIVE

Bar Chart Showing The Town or Village Where People Live

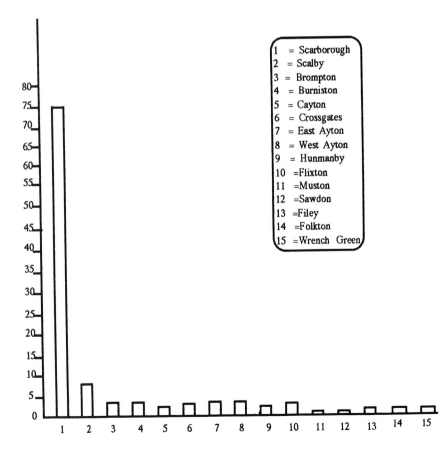

CENSUS - SCARBOROUGH

SECTION 1 : WHERE YOU LIVE

GROUP MEMBERS   Virgina, Adele and Victoria

Question 5: Please give the ward in which you live.

Not all the people answered the census form we sent out. We received 112 forms back but only 94 answered this particular question. This is 84%. We think this was maybe because they did not know which ward they lived in.

Weaponness had the majority which is not surprising because Weaponness is the Ward in which St. Martin's Schools is in.

18 families out of 94 (which is 19%) live in Weaponness parish.

By Virginia and Victoria

SECTION **1** :   WHERE YOU LIVE

A Bar Chart Showing The Ward In Which People Live

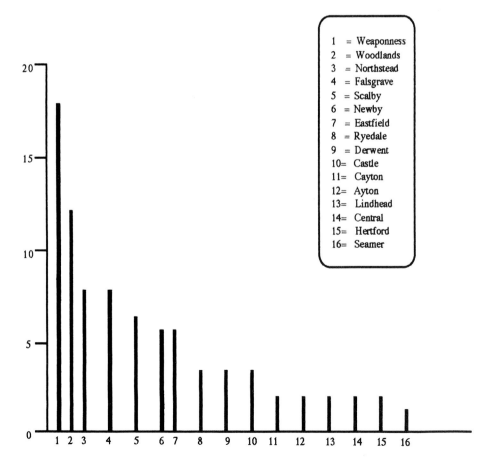

```
1  = Weaponness
2  = Woodlands
3  = Northstead
4  = Falsgrave
5  = Scalby
6  = Newby
7  = Eastfield
8  = Ryedale
9  = Derwent
10= Castle
11= Cayton
12= Ayton
13= Lindhead
14= Central
15= Hertford
16= Seamer
```

SECTION 1: WHERE YOU LIVE

A Bar Chart Showing How Many Questionnaires

We Each Typed Onto the QUEST Database

by Virginia

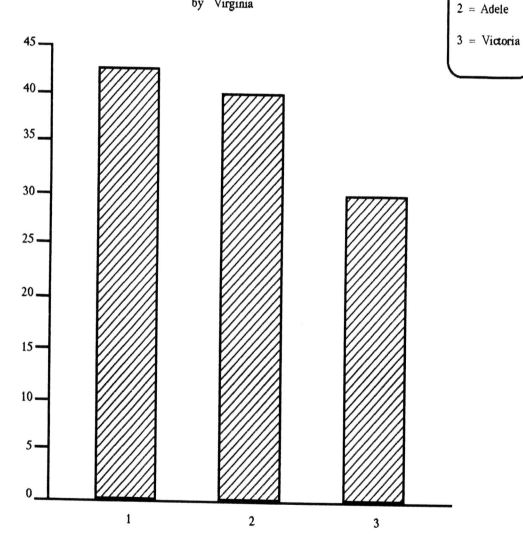

1 = Virginia

2 = Adele

3 = Victoria

Chapter 9
"1588"—An Approach Utilising Information Technology
Joyce I. Fields

This article serves to illustrate how Information Technology contributed towards a link-curricular topic on The Spanish Armada of 1588, with a class of Year Four and Year Five children. This project gathered so much momentum and produced so much enthusiasm that it extended well over a term and a half, exploring avenues could neither have been anticipated nor envisaged.

The topic, the Spanish Armada of 1588, was approached in a thematic link-curricular mode. For ease of reference I have identified main subject headings making it possible to extract individual areas for discussion, clarification and evaluation. It would be impossible to detail every aspect of the work covered in this short article, therefore, a brief overview must suffice.

Information Technology may be interpreted as using a computer as an invaluable means of storage, of retrieving data and/or as a means of drafting and editing written work, but in its fuller sense 'Information Technology' includes the use of the video camera and video, and audio equipment such as cassette recorders, music centres, record players, keyboards, synthesizers, and also calculators. In addition to this wider interpretation word processing, spreadsheets, databases, *Dart, LOGO,* simulations and adventure games were all deemed relevant in their use within the chosen topic, because of the skills which they encourage in the field of problem solving, collaboration, discussion and planning, and because of their content free open ended investigational properties. These media were, therefore, used as an integral part of the planning.

The ideas, examples and suggestions described here may enable readers to see the possibilities for curriculum enrichment in their own classrooms through Information Technology.

Aims

Through using a well-known historical event, the main aims were to provide the following:

a. an opportunity for each individual child to develop at his/her own speed thus fulfilling his/her own potential without experiencing a sense of inadequacy or failure.

b. facilities for the children to promote their own ideas in a free creative manner.

c. an opportunity, through working in groups, to develop collaborative skills in problem solving and decision making.

d. an involvement in group decision making to heighten the children's awareness for the need to consider others and their points of view.

e. an opportunity for the children effectively to organise their own activities over an extended period of time.

f. the opportunity to develop the skills involved in finding information from a variety of sources, disseminating this information, and reporting back to class members.

Organisation and Management

To achieve the above, much consideration had to been given to organisation, management and resourcing within the classroom a crucial factor in the success of the undertaking. The need to have access to relevant equipment was of as important, as its positioning and availability.

The basic organisation of the class was that of small groups enabling children to develop a more collaborative approach to their work. The development of the social interaction became most interesting as the children soon began to realise the need for advanced planning of future activities, as well as the need for planning an effective distribution of the workload. Talking and listening were perceived as high status activities, wherein different dialogue strategies could be used to extend and sustain the children's use of language.

A variety of classroom management issues connected with specific elements of the topic had to be considered – assessment problems; management of time; children's familiarity with equipment, allowing for independent usage and selection of appropriate software and pursuing work appropriate to their attainment level.

Likewise, the strategies employed in trial and error situations developed as individual activities gathered momentum. The most noticeable immediate factor was the ways in which individual independence grew. Enabling the children to be self-selecting in the suite of programs they felt appropriate to their own individual needs, as opposed to the software packages dictating their curriculum. I must stress my fortunate position at not having the constraints of time-tabling one computer work-station into rigid time slots for availability and usage.

All areas of the curriculum played an important role in this topic, with little imbalance of input. The teacher's role became, in effect, one of facilitator and co-ordinator responsible for ensuring continuity between all the events and activities.

Curriculum Areas

The subject areas covered were:

- **Language Development Skills**

A video of a Shakespearian play helped to establish the concept of time-lapse and exposed the children to the appropriate mode of dress, idiom of speech, and social graces. It was a valuable experience. Through 'role play' based on the 'Time Travellers', groups of children armed with tape recorders and video recorders assumed the role of newspaper reporters and television newscasters. Their assignment was to relate the preparatory events leading up to the outcome of the Spanish Armada based on authentic details and information collected from the video and other reference sources.

In this guise, a range of articles was written by the children using computer software packages such as *Fleet Street Editor, Wordwise Plus, Storywriter, Typesetter*, and *Easywrite*, displaying a range of language modes: expressive, transaction and poetic. The media resulted in the children's confident and sympathetic involvement in this language work.

Using desk top publishing program facilities for display materials, banner headlines, display notices, and signs two competitive class newspapers were set up. Each newspaper reported and announced discoveries; produced articles pertaining to the events of the day as seen through the eyes of the role model and reported on the variety of on-going activities within the classroom. Without the flexibility of the facilities available on the *Fleet Street Editor, Typesetter and Wordwise Plus* suites of software packages, the results would not have been so effective, or so efficient, as the children wrote and published imaginary letters describing sea voyages, fears, battles, cruelty, conversations (written and verbal).

The tape recorder and video proved to be invaluable teaching aids establishing empathy and clarity of well-reasoned arguments. The need for slow, clear diction and audibility of speech in reading in phases to make for true understanding of their 'news' items, was greatly appreciated.

At times some children displayed frustration with the reference books available, because they were either insufficiently detailed or they were far beyond the children's comprehension and understanding. To resolve this situation parents were enlisted to type in the relevant facts in a simplified form. This allowed for ease of access to such information. Software packages such as *Typesetter, Wordwise Plus, Junior View* and *Grasshopper* spreadsheets were used allowing the children to develop their own plot and extract the main facts, details and characters based on authentic historical detail.

As the children were highly motivated their ability to retrieve this information developed rapidly, as did their ability to correctly and effectively use indexes, content indicators in reference books and the classification system used in the school and Military camp libraries. These skills were quickly acquired as it proved to be a good opportunity for the children to learn life skills needed in organisation, co-operation, sequencing, and planning. Out of necessity the execution of battle scenes and fight sequences had to have pre-determined moves.

More able children used *PenDown* to create their individual adventure stories based on their perceptions of the events of the Spanish Armada, while the needs of less able children were enhanced by much usage of the Concept Keyboard and concept keyboard overlays using *Prompt Writer 3*. Much drafting and redrafting of the narratives and articles was achieved through using appropriate software packages, as was the development of the understanding that writing is an on-going process focusing into the widening breadth and depth of vocabulary, not a 'once and for all activity'. Similar skills were learnt by the groups engaged in producing diaries of the events; captains' logs; pretending to be historians recording events as they happened; song writers and poets.

The screen dump program *Snatch* was extremely useful enabling the children to print out pictures or text or a combination of both, before adding their own ideas to produce 'news' items or booklets. With the multi-copy facilities on the computers it was easy to make several copies of their work into illustrated books. Each child having his/her own copy, one being placed on the classroom library shelf, and one being sent home.

Utilising the vast amount of information collected *Infant Tray* and *Easywrite* were used to produce appropriate relevant text in a variety of forms *viz.* cloze procedures, word searches, crosswords.

On-going throughout the topic the children's ability to read, effectively scan, and trace work done by other groups pursuing appropriate activities, enabled the children to appreciate their contribution to the whole outcome and have a greater understanding of the whole topic. It was essential to have regular whole class discussion sessions, yielded opportunities for teacher assessment of group and individual development.

- **Maths**
  The following is a summary of some of the mathematical investigation initiated and developed using electronic calculators and various software computer packages.

  Calculators were used to re-arrange the date 1588 into doubling, halving, spiral numbers, highest and lowest possible sequences, subtraction, addition, multiplication, division in magic squares. Likewise exploratory activities for telling the time, analogue and digital; the science of the mechanics of timepieces leading onto making water clocks, sand clocks, and candle clocks, antique timepieces, and accurate calibrations. As did activities involving directions, bearings, co-ordinates; reading scales, using a fathom mark, thermometer work, barometers, Beaufort scale. Money experiences involved coin value, handling money as change, shopping, costing of large items with graph pictorial representations. As with the measurement of distances and size, wind speeds; making clinometers, astrolabes and other navigational instruments.

  The use of electronic calculators made the most significant contribution to this development of mathematical concepts and understandings, because through their use the children were able to confidently and accurately tackle complex mathematical investigational work. Not only did the children gain considerable competence in these mathematical processes by making accurate repeated calculations, they also developed positive attitudes towards mathematical investigations in general.

  One group of children set up a business 'Tudor Supersave' utilising light sensors to keep an on-going record of produce sold using *Grasshopper* database for stock-taking and for working out profits. The children organised the layout of their shop, along with the costings, monies, turnovers, collated expenditures, equipment and job descriptions required for the year. These activities were linked to Art and Craft techniques of using plaster of Paris to make cakes, bread, and these items were displayed in the fashion of a street market stall.

Through an activity on symmetry, involving paper cutting and quilling to create Elizabethan Knot Gardens, the children were able to explore the attributes of shapes such as their position, rotation, reflection and translation in symmetry movements using *LOGO and Dart*. Their understanding of the idea of angle measurement of angular rotation in degrees was enhanced as was its relevance to link activities such as the practical context of compass work and the plotting of bearings. The idea of effectively measuring with scale and symbolic representation in mapping skills and co-ordinates linked naturally to three dimensional map work covered in geographical skills and in Art and Craft.

Timers, water clocks, sand clocks and candle clocks, were devised and much effort went into the refining of designs as a result of calibrating them with an electronic digital timer. Suitable 'fair test' experiments were repeated and their results plotted in graph form, thus introducing elementary ideas of range and valid statistical samples.

A working plan to the scaled measurement of a galleon based on the Macdonalds Publication kit was plotted in the school playground. This contributed to the development of a concept of the length and the height of a galleon illustrating the volume of space required for the storage of the quantity of provisions needed for a full compliment of men. Although the sinking of King Henry VIII's flagship, the *Mary Rose* happened some forty years earlier than the Armada, the simulation program *Mary Rose* proved to be very useful and manageable with adult support. Provisions and stores from the ship's manifesto provided relevant and interesting data to be collated. For instance the distribution of food and drink rations were extremely meagre, in relation to the many hours of hard work the sailors were expected to achieve. Visits to the school canteen kitchen and the loyal Royal Engineers field kitchen were arranged to underpin the concepts of weight and quantity in comparative provisions. Cooking traditional Spanish dishes involved measuring and weighing of ingredients resulting in mathematical skills becoming a cultural experience. Much discussion as to the variety of diet and dishes lead to the presentation of this information on recipes, ingredients and instructions in 'Mrs. Drake's Cookery Book'.

Using these details problem solving activities arose related to food consumption, costing, dietary requirements, economic methods of storing and cooking. From this the children were able to develop various theories as to the total overall cost of the Armada campaign. The plotting of graphs using recordings of the data for the food storage, water requirements, materials for repairs to armaments etc. lead onto scientific experiments, such as the length of time the ships took to sail from Cadiz loaded down with provisions in comparison to the length of time they took to sail round Scotland and Ireland with much lighter loads. The children conclusions being that this in part lead to the ships not being as stable as the provision acted as ballasts. This fact, compounded with the extreme weather conditions, contributed to the disastrous results.

LOGO writing procedures ensured and maintained the interest of the more able children whose project was to make the turtle follow the Armada route on a map in the correct sequence of events. Also, using precise programming skills, they had to demonstrate the Spanish method of 'tracking' against the oncoming winds. This resulted in a map of the continent and the British Isles being drawn onto acetate, and secured to the visual display unit.

Simplified exercises using *Touch explorer* were devised enabling less able children to find relevant details of the sequence of events, as well as giving them the opportunity to add their own researched data, such as the Battle of Gravelines and the names and dates of the ships lost. The end result of this work was a 'An Armada Book of Events'.

Much mathematical work was achieved by turning a work area into an Elizabethan Dock resulting in the construction of jibs, quays, barrels, etc. The link with historical and geographical aspects were languages, currencies, size comparison of countries, and other relevant data which was placed on the retrieval systems. This enabled the children to plot simplified graphs of population sizes comparing relative English village populations to an estimated military populations in various Army camps in West Germany, where our school was situated.

• **Science**

The length of time spent by the children experimenting with the various elements in the following investigations in science will be appreciated in the context of their link-curricular mode.

Based on a problem solving activity originated by Mr. G. Wright, Deputy Headteacher, Wheatcroft Primary School, Scarborough, the children had to raise the *Mary Rose* from the bottom of a fish tank using levers and pulleys. This was done in conjunction with the simulation program the *Mary Rose*.

This work lead onto a variety of experiments into the maximum efficiency of the wind effects on the design of the shape and the size of sails; the height of the castles built on the galleons causing them to become unstable and capsize, the stability and draught of the structure of the keel, the need for ballasts for stability. The height of the castles influenced the stability of the vessels as the children found the ships did not sail particularly well and that they pitched and rolled making them slow and difficult to manoeuvre. This was overcome when the children made the hulls narrower in relation to the width of the decks: resulting in the hulls being almost shaped like fish, causing effective fast manoeuvrability.

The trajectory and effectiveness of canon balls was investigated because from the historical sources it was found that sixteenth century canon balls were very inaccurate over a distance of about two hundred metres. The children constructed elastic band propelled catapult canons to test the effects of shooting ball bearings at targets made from a variety of woods. This was linked to mathematical activities such as the plotting of graphs: ratio of weight to distance plus effectiveness.

Tension and strength experiments on the structure of ropes were exciting as the children were able to vary their parameters to work out the thickness of string in ratio to the number of twists required to ascertain the ropes maximum weight bearing capacity. This experimentation was also carried out to find which was considered to be the best material to use – cotton, nylon, a mixture, twill, wool, and whether being wet changed the properties and the structure efficiency of the ropes.

Many interesting experiments were devised to ascertain the effectiveness of the manoeuvrability of the four wheeled canon carriages, which the English used in comparison to the manoeuvrability of the two wheeled canon carriage the Spanish used. Resulting in the four wheeled canon carriages proving more stable in their construction, which may have been a deciding factor in the effect of success of failure in battle.

Much interest in stars and navigation was generated so the children linked their science skills and experiments with a variety of activities whilst telescopes, 'eye glasses', kaleidoscopes, sun-dials, navigation instruments, using various computer programs involving navigation, stars and co-ordinates.

Developing on from this work, related to compasses and the plotting of bearings, the children made simple compasses using a long macrame 'T' pin, secured in a round cork, for the pivot and magnets to magnetise thin pieces of iron or steel, which were suspended on top of the 'T' pin.

Another activity related to salvage work on the Armada wrecks, in order to recover the valuable bronze guns and jewellery on board the Spanish ships, lead to numerous experiments in designing and testing various diving bells fashioned on the principle of the 'Tobermory Galleon bell'.

Numerous lengths of piping were used to make tuned tubular bells as well as using water in bottles to make tuned musical sequences, and hose pipes and funnels to make musical instruments with a trumpet-like sound. All of the above contributed to the final production of the children's assembly "Fire over England" a link-curricular approach where much imaginative writing was produced from their work on survival after being shipwrecked.

- **Humanities**

In the geographical aspects of the topic many skills were developed through the following comparisons of England in relation to the British Isles, Spain, seas, world map, capital cities, European map, places relevant to the Armada, map readings, drawing and making three dimensional maps showing geographical features, circumnavigation, flat map to globe, languages, currencies, size comparison of countries, populations relative to England and Army camps in Germany, climatic conditions, and reasons for the Armada.

This was inter-related through using historical facts found in reference sources already cited to demonstrate a visual understanding of their sequence of events by plotting this historical data onto a three dimensional model of the British Isles and the Continent. Through this method the geographical relationships of places of interest in the events of the Spanish Armada were clearly and visually shown. Creative writing based on authentic facts and about events enabled the children to empathise and relate their own experience to the life styles prevalent during the 1580s. These naturally arose from the children 'role play' of historical characters and events using other subject areas. Incidental learning took place through the children's own travelling experiences as they were able to identify the places visited.

The children engaged in a selection of link-curriculum activities such as compass work, the plotting of bearings, an elementary understanding of geographical features influencing historical outcomes, and reasons for towns and cities developing; plotting of graphs and voyages; mode of dress and reasons for certain articles of clothing such as high heeled shoes for men as well as women; gentlemen always walked to the outside or left of their ladies in order to be able to defend them with their sword arm; banquets in comparison to meagre meals for the poor; comparing eating utensils of 1580s with utensils of 1980s such as two prong forks with four prong forks; comparing present day items with those of four hundred years ago *viz* plastic items with pewter items; ironing facilities with then and now – flat iron compared to modern steam electric iron; cleaning brushes compared with willow brooms; effectiveness of straw ovens against microwave ovens; building materials and method of construction of homes and houses lead onto a sub-topic of looking at building within our local German community. In particular analysing their initial use with their changed usages over time. For example, a local monastery in Germany was built in circa 1588, used as a bonded warehouse and partly derelict during circa 1880s and restored before being used as a palatial hotel with exclusive departmental stores in the 1980s.

Other historical aspects covered included areas such as artefacts – pottery olive jars, bosun's whistle, bronze navigational dividers, bronze astrolabes, wooden linstock which held a burning taper to fire the canons, magnificent paintings. tapestries, jewellery, armour and weapons; preparing an archeological dig-logical order of events, apparatus required, made own facsimiles, and replicas; Chatham Chest which held contributions for a benevolent fund to help the sick and wounded.

As historians have argued that the importance of the Armada campaign has been exaggerated and opposed to the popular belief that the English totally defeated the Spanish during the Armada campaign, much discussion in terms of 'moral' education ensued. This heightened the children's awareness that popular conceptions of glorifying wars are not necessarily based on true historical detail. They were provided with opportunities to disseminate the truth of the campaign from the myth that had grown up over the years.

Using historical documents the children learnt that nearly two thirds of the original force of one hundred and fifty warships bearing 30,693 returned safely to Spain. Those who escaped the storms were executed by the Scots and the Irish. The popular belief that the English sailors came home to cheering crowds after being rewarded for their courage, was far from the reality of a more complex situation. Sick and dying men were discharged onto the streets, without pay, after the campaign. Illness and disease were widespread throughout both fleets resulting from the unhealthy cramped conditions.

The bases for 'moral' education, as for all learning, is an on-going learning process. So 'every war has its casualties and every victory its price' was extensively discussed in a sensitive manner. As this was a delicate situation it was gently worked through with the children using 'role play', as they lived within a military atmosphere.

- **Art and Craft**

Much of the Art and Craft work dealt with the making and the production of props and costumes needed for the class Assembly play entitled "Fire over England".

Using a variety of media such as empty packages of breakfast cereals, cardboard, kitchen foil, tie dyed materials, buttons, split pins, ink dyes etc. the children made authentic looking Spanish helmets, armour, banners, shields, swords, England bloomer-type costumes, plumed hats, for the various participants of the play.

As the interest in Elizabethan Knot Gardens developed much interesting work was explored in Art and Craft as described in Mathematic section. Having sketched, drawn, painted examples of these the children experimented with a variety of materials to gain a three dimensional effect. The most successful of these being the use of 'Quilling'. *LOGO and Dart* computer programs proved most useful as it was possible to develop the children's acquired skills further by placing acetate over the visual display unit. Their task was initially to build programs which would match the complexity of the design on the acetate. This was then printed out and used as the template for the three dimensional models of Elizabethan Knot Gardens. Some of the patterns were so intricate and pleasing to look at that the children decided to enlarge or decrease them, in order that they could be used as repeated patterns in block printing to print a display drape or for book covers.

With the wide range of materials available the children became quite sophisticated in choosing the best medium for individual pieces of art work, such as chalk shadowed crayoning pictures; shadow silhouettes which were fashionable during those days; block printing and a variety of lino prints matched to the quilling pattern; coloured water marks for the inside covers of bookbinding whilst making their own book covers; splatter and bubble painting with oil based paints which was common during the c1560s; applique collage type work, cross stitch sampler work which was also popular; ropes full of various smelling herbs and lavender were made with the help and expertise of a helping mother, who had experience in the use of herbs. This developed into the children learning about the importance of herbs and herbal cures in the 1580s—alternative medicine.

The children designed and mounted much of their own display work which were carefully and minutely detailed within the style of Elizabethan type borders typical of the border techniques used during the Armada. These activities were closely linked to the children's Mathematical investigations on symmetry and repeated pattern tasks.

Initially we used a model galleon from a kit produced by Macdonalds Publications to gain an insight into the differing elements and functions of the various parts of the galleon. The children were soon developing their own designs, which lead onto some most interesting science experimental work which is discussed under that subject area.

It was felt that to develop the historical and geographical aspects further that a three dimensional model of an Elizabethan map could be made using Modroc. Much mess and pleasure ensued as the children made a scaled model of the British Isles and the coastline of Holland, France, Portugal and Spain on top of a tracing of an old map upon which the route of the Armada was displayed with model ships.

As the skills of the blacksmith were essential to the making and maintenance of the canons and arms on the galleons, we visited the Blues and Royals Regimental blacksmiths workshop to watch the fashioning of heated metal into various items. The regimental carpenter, also, very kindly showed the children some of the techniques and tools used in the carving and polishing of wood. This led to the children using *LOGO and Dart* programs to make their own patterns and carvings, which the children attempted in sculpturing clay or plasticine.

Some very interest intricate drawings of galleons. Costumes, and imaginary scenes for a 'Tudor Shadow Theatre' using *AMX Paint Pot and Super Art* were produced. Because the computer facilities made it possible to rotate, reflect and copy the design, once it has been transferred to the screen, the children produced designs for books covers, pseudo-Elizabethean tiles and wallpaper. This allowed the children freedom of expression using other creative media.

- **Expressive Arts**

Considerable time was spent composing music and experimenting with various 'Maypole' type dances, and other dance routines, plus fight sequences, before the children achieved a satisfying end result for their production.

They made their own instruments using tea chests/cones, rubber stretched over large cans from the kitchen, elastic bands over cylinders, boxes, water in bottles, etc. involving many of the concepts and skills required in science. Initially, the children started by comparing familiar modern pop songs to recordings of early Tudor music performed mainly on lyres, crump horns, zithers etc. To gain approximations to the sounds heard the children chose tambourines as their timbrels but placed various thicknesses of cloth over certain areas to achieve a mixture of a drum/tambourine sound. The children also experimented with their recorders by inserting varying sizes of cones to get a close approximation to the more reedy tones of the crump horn and early Tudor recorder sounds.

This lead onto using the computer program *Compose* which has preset phrases of English, Chinese and Indian style music, allowing the user to build his/her own sequence of tunes. This was used with a view to the children writing their own introductory music for their class assembly performance. The children used the video and the cassette recorder to record the sections of music which they felt to be most appropriate. But it was very soon realised that although *Compose* was found initial to be a very good starting point it was too restrictive and had too many constraints, preventing an authentic sounding mood of early Tudor reed musical sounds.

So it was necessary to explore possibilities of the Software package *Music*. The children were able to work out the notation from xylophones, pianos, etc. onto traditional notation staves, which the computer played back. Using an interface box linked to a MIDI system synthesizers were combined to the computer allowing the children to add drums and reed sounding type instruments into the background. They were able to create, store and retrieve their edited tunes.

Throughout the topic the children were introduced to as wide a variety of classical music as was possible. On hearing the canons being fired in the *1812' Overture* the children felt they wanted something similar in their music. They devised many ways of using corrugated sheets or sheets of thin metal to get similar sounds, because they found that recording authentic gun salutes did not sound as effective.

It was interesting to share the children's perceptions and interpretations of the *Karelia Suite* by Sibelius, which suggested to them sailors excitedly rushing up and down the rigging of the galleons in preparation for the ensuing battles.

Sea and wind sounds were created by blowing down variety of different sized cardboard tubes, and vocalising splashing wave sounds, which were edited into authentic sea and wind recordings.

Colleagues suffered uncomplainingly during the children's attempts to make their own music, which was at times the most dreadful cacophony of noise.

All this exploratory work resulted in a reasonably pleasant sounding victory march with a happy jilting march speed, full of trumpets and steady drum beats illustrating a positive forward advance of the English troops based on the 'Great Gate of Kiev'. This was clearly in contrast to the unenthusiastic march developed by another group of children, demonstrating a depressed forlonged mood illustrating despair and defeat of the Spanish.

Lots of relevant activities arose from the above, and were developed from the story content before being expressed in various features of choral speaking, movement, physical education and drama. These activities were noisy and fraught but very purposeful and pleasurable.

Summary

Our experiences opened new vistas where Information Technology totally integrated and supported every aspect of the on-going work production in an established curriculum. This proved to be an invaluable asset, not in a contrived, artificial manner but as a genuine need for the facilities and powerful use of Information Technology.

The whole project was very worthwhile as the feedback from the children and their parents reaffirmed that the best way for children to learn in a meaningful manner, is for them to be actively involved in initiating their own programmes of study.

We went,
We saw
We felt,
and if you
[child, adult, teacher, visitor]
are sufficiently interested
you too can learn
what we discovered.

Pluckrose H. 'Children in their Primary School.'

Further Reading:

Arkell, t. (1989) Analysing Victorian Census Data on Computer. *Teaching History* January, pp. 18–25.

Blenkin, G. and Kelly, A. V. (1987) *The Primary Curriculum*. Harper and Row

Crompton, R. (1989) *Computers and the Primary Curriculum*. Falmer Press.

DES (1989) *Information Technology from 5 to 16. Curriculum Matters* 15, HMSO.

DES (1990) *Technology in the National Curriculum*. HMSO

NCET (1989) *Using Technologies in History*. NCET, University of Warwick Science Park, Conventry,

Papert, S. (1980) *Mindstorms: Children, Computers and Powerful ideas*. Harvester Press.

Phillips, M. (1990) For the record. *Educational Computing and Technology*, March.

Straker, A. (1989) *Children Using Computers*, Blackwell.

Chapter 10

Music Technology with Pupils with Severe Learning Difficulties

Rod Buckle

Making music has always traditionally been a valued part of the curriculum in schools for pupils with severe learning difficulties. Because of the physical and cognitive problems displayed by these children this has usually been restricted to the shaking of washing up bottles containing peas or simple percussion instruments. The child's perceptual and hapto-kinesthetic abilities tend to dictate the quality and direction that any music making activity takes. In many schools children are within the school framework from the age of two up to nineteen years. This increases the problems of motivation and in providing a valued and meaningful program of music making activities. Most of the musical activities tend to have a high content of rote learning of motor skills and little (if any) creativity. Children are constrained by their limitations rather than being encouraged to by-pass them and concentrate on what they can achieve as individuals. It has long been accepted that because of their severe learning difficulties, often linked to a degree of physical/perceptual difficulties, these children have not been able to create or perform music. With the advent of the new technology, synthesiser keyboards linked to a computer can enable children to overcome their perceptual and physical limitations and create high quality sound responses for very little physical or cognitive input. With the most handicapped pupils this technological approach to music will encourage them to make physical movement or to come to realise the effect their movement is creating, as part of both a creative and therapeutic process. The sounds and phrases are already set up within the instruments and can be released, experimented with the finally put together to create a finished piece of music by all pupils.

Obviously the decision whether to commit a large investment of both money and time commitment was not one to be taken lightly. As I had little musical ability and even less experience of synthesisers, this entailed myself and colleagues learning hand in hand with the children involved. This proved to be no problem in fact, was seen as a positive bonus. A trip to a local secondary school to see what synthesisers were capable of revealed that they would not only achieve the desired effect for our pupils but were easy to use for people like myself with limited knowledge of music.

Before making a large investment I approached a professional musician who agreed to bring a number of synthesisers into school and work with a range of pupils to gauge pupil reaction. The funding towards this day was provided in part by

95

Yorkshire Arts for which I was grateful. The response of all the pupils who worked with the electronic instruments showed that this was the direction we needed to explore. We took advice from a number of sources and searched for advantageous prices of the right kind of equipment for our needs.

A group of local professional musicians heard of our plans and raised a large amount of money which was supplemented by funds also raised in the local area and equipment was purchased. The equipment consisted of the following:

Yamaha PSS 480 synthesiser which contains a programmable drum machine which enables pupils to build up complex drum rhythms beat by beat. This means that providing a child can tap a key once they can create a realistic sounding drum track without necessarily having the motor control normally associated with this kind of activity. The keyboard also contains one hundred programmed accompaniment rhythms which can be chosen at the touch of a button along with a selection of one hundred different instrument voices. As each rhythm and voice can be manipulated by simple key presses along with frequency and tone modulation one does not need to be a mathematician to see that the range of creative possibilities available to pupils is vast.

YAMAHA P50 voice sampler and keyboard. This contains many of the more "fun" type of facilities. A pupil can record an external sound into the keyboards microphone, including a sound created by their voice, and then add a number of "effects". They can add echo to their spoken name and sound as though they are in a vast cave, they can play tunes using their names, or they can make it play backwards etc. Their voice can be made high pitched to sound like "Mickey Mouse" or low pitched to sound like a monster. A useful facility for pupils with poor motor co-ordination is being able to record one clap of the hands. This can then be easily multiplied and produced in many rhythms which would normally prove to be very difficult, if not impossible, for many of our children.

TASCAN 05 Portastudio This is a multi-track recording machine which enables a child to record each part of his creation (with adult help). This can then be played back whilst a second part is created, practised and finally recorded as a second track. If necessary this process can be continued until ten tracks have been recorded. A high quality stereo recording can be obtained at the end of the process. This allows the pupils to create their own high quality recordings which can be used in the dance sessions the children take part in as part of the school curriculum. The children can then create their own movement interpretations of their musical creations and complete a totally self generated creative process.

All the equipment is fed through a high quality amplifier and two large one hundred watt speaker enclosures. This not only ensures a "realism" quality to the created instrument sounds but enables partially sighted pupils to "feel" the sound through the speaker grills. The sound levels can be increased for pupils with a hearing loss and a number of headphones can be connected to the equipment for the most able pupils who may be working in small groups creating rhythms and melodies ready for recording, the whole area has been organised to allow easy access for pupils in wheelchairs.

A computer is coupled to the synthesisers and operates a light synthesiser which enables either the teacher or the pupils to create light shows onto a television screen.

These consists of multi-coloured light displays which can include fountain/waterfall effects, floating patterns, bird shapes, lightning and cascading coloured lights which can be made to move, change colour or pulsate to the music being played by simple keyboard presses. As well as offering a creative process for the more able pupils it offers the opportunity for a highly motivational and pleasurable experience for our more profoundly handicapped pupils.

Why do we teach sound creation? I feel music is a multisensory experience. Seeing, moving and listening are all important ingredients of any music curriculum, making music a natural way of enhancing and developing sensory perception and psychomotor skills. Children actually learn to learn through music creation activities. It can help to develop skills that are necessary for cognitive, affective and psychomotor functioning utilized in all areas of the school curriculum. Unlike activities which rely on verbal interaction sound creation rarely fails to communicate in some way with every child. In addition, because of the flexibility of approach available in music, a single activity can include children of widely differing abilities. Sound creation enables every intellect to be challenged no matter how inhibited. Children who are unable or unwilling to verbalise their feelings and ideas can fine a freedom to express themselves in unfettered ways. Music technology supplements teaching methodologies by providing a different medium through which other teaching aims can be refined and ultimately reinforced. For pupils such as ours achievement in creating music, no matter how small, can reaffirm a sense of worth as well as improve general functioning.

As this approach within our school is in it's infancy the learning process is developing with each session which passes. Pupils create sounds and rhythms not envisaged by teachers. Children's imaginations are not dictated to by any pre-conceived ideas of the "correct" way of doing things by "expert" adults. The learning experience is enjoyed and broadened by all participants be they teachers or pupils. However certain learning skills and objectives can be noted. The following areas will probably be extended and widened as the project develops.

APPENDIX:

Sound Creation Learning Skills/Objectives

Auditory Perception

Sound awareness	*sound/noise/silence*
Sound location	*where is it coming from?*
Sound discrimination/dynamic same/different	*loud/soft*
	long/short
	fast/slow
	beat patterns
	high/low
	up/down
Listening skills	*auditory memory*
	auditory sequencing
Visual perception	*awareness clues/gestures*
Visual focus	*locates instrument*
	focuses on lights
	focuses on teacher
Visual tracking	*follows lights/teacher*
Visual discrimination	*colour/shape/size/quantity/*
	direction/ distance
Visual memory	*recognition same/different*
Motor skills	*fine/gross motor*
Language skills	*vocalisation*
	expressive language
	receptive language
	articulation rhythms
Social skills	*self concept*
	co-operation
	attention span
	motivation levels
	peer group relations
	adult relations
	predict outcomes
	value judgements
	pleasure

References:

DES 919780 *Special Educational Needs [Warnock Report]* London: HMSO.

HMI 91990a0 *Special Educational Needs in Initial Teacher Training London*: HMSO.

HMI [1990b] *Special Needs Issues. London*: HMSO

NCC [1989] *A Curriculum for All: Special Educational Needs in the National Curriculum* York: National Curriculum Council.

Roaf, C. & Bines , H. [eds.] [1989] *Needs, Rights and Opportunities: Developing Approaches to Special Education*. Lewes: Falmer Press.

Chapter 11
"Movement": A Science Curriculum File Supported by Information Technology

Alison Drage

As a teacher with 18 years experience, my current interest is in IT & Science with ethnic minority children in Southall, W. London.

Equal opportunities is a principle the school in which I work is very committed. This can be very difficult to achieve in IT and science for two reasons: firstly, IT and science is often seen to be performed by white men in white coats using complicated language and secondly physical science is often seen as "boys" topics. Frequently, the boys have had much more experience at home playing with Lego, electrical toys etc. and are more confident in handling mechanical equipment. Consequently, the boys take over the micro-computers and all the best equipment and the girls become passive onlookers, reluctant and/or frightened to handle the equipment. Not only are equal opportunities an issue to be considered in the classroom but also, economic awareness and citizenship issues must be addressed. This places an even greater burden on the over stretched class teacher. With these factors in mind the planning and organising of the work is very important. In my experience very few teachers feel confident in developing a balanced information technology and science programme for their class. However, by law every class teacher now has to provide such programmes for each child.

The National Curriculum places further burdens and can be divided into two parts: Attainment Target 1 which outlines the processes that children should go through at each stage and Attainment Targets 2–4 which details the content which should be taught. However, these Attainment Targets are not, in my opinion, developmental. Attainment Target 1 may appear at first glance to be simplistic but many teachers seem not to have really grasped the implications of this Attainment Target and often tend to present science as filling the answers on a worksheet. An approach which is entirely devoid of investigative and exploratory process. This attainment target is worth about 50% of the marks in the testing of the S.A.T.s.

Whilst writing a science curriculum file for the Reception, Years 1 and 2, 5-7 year olds, much time was spent asking first school colleagues where they felt they needed more resources. Generally their opinions were in agreement that on the whole they covered a lot of biological science and felt able to develop this successfully. However, it was felt that although infant and first school children did a lot of physical science the teachers were not confident in developing the activities beyond a superficial level. With this in mind a concept frequently avoided by primary teachers— namely forces was chosen as the bases for the science curriculum file.

The Science National Curriculum is divided up into 4 Attainment targets. Attainment Target 4 is named 'Physical processes' which includes "forces" and the requirements for Reception, Years 1 and 2, 5–7 year olds are

1.   Know that things can be moved by pushing them.

2.   Understand that pushes and pulls can make things start moving, speed up swerve or stop.

3.   Understand that when things are changed in shape, begin to move or stop moving, forces are acting on them.

4.   Understand the factors which cause objects to float or sink in water.

An obvious topic that looks at 'forces' in detail is "movement", which is a topic very easily handled by young children. It is difficult to cover a topic on movement without looking at energy. The Science Attainment Target 4 is Energy and the Statement of Attainment level 3a states that: "children should understand in qualitative terms, that models and machines need a source of energy in order to work". Also the National Curriculum programmes of study and the paragraph which embraces Attainment Target 4 states that:

"In the context of classroom and outdoor play activities, children should experience natural and manufactured forces which push, pull, make things move, stop things and change the shape of objects. Such experiences could include, for example, road safety activities."

The paragraph concerning Attainment Target 4 has a sentence which is relevant to a topic on "movement". It states that "children should have early experience with devices, for e.g. toys which move and store energy."

One of the most important Attainment Targets in the Science National Curriculum is Attainment Target 1 as its recommendations is presented and carried out in the classroom for every topic. *Viz:*

1.   Observe familiar materials and events in their immediate environment, at first hand, using their senses.

     Describe and communicate their observations ideally through talking in groups or by other means, within their class.

2.   Ask questions and suggest ideas of the how, why and what will happen if variety.

     Identify simple differences, for e.g., hot/cold, rough/smooth. Use non-standard and standard measures, for e.g., hand-spans and rulers.

     List and collate observations.

     Interpret findings by associating one factor with another, for e.g., the pupils perception at this level that "light objects float", "thin wood is bendy".

     Record findings in charts, drawings and other appropriate forms.

All these processes are undertaken naturally in all good infant classrooms.

At the outset the planning of the topic on 'movement' began with a topic web. The topic on, 'movement' naturally fell into 3 distinct areas—moving on land, moving through water and moving through air encompassing the usual activities carried out in infant and first school classes, for e.g. playing with balls, toys, water play balloons and paper aeroplanes.

The next problem tackled was to decide on the best layout of the teachers notes so that they were:

a. clearly laid out and easy to read
b. developmental questions to ask the children
c. ideas on the activities that the children could undertake from the questions
d. links with the three core subject areas for ease of recording teachers aid sheets to help them make the science equipment and models
e. worksheets for the children
f. a list of resources they need to collect

Taking each of these criteria individually it was found that:

- The work had to be clearly laid out and in simple every day language so as to take away the assumed 'mysteries' of science.
- The work had to be developmental as many reference books have very good ideas as starting off points but lack the ideas to help teachers develop the topic confidently.
- Questions to ask children.

The latter criterion may seem a strange inclusion for teachers. Although teachers ask questions all the time, it is very important, however, to ask correct questions which give children confidence in developing their own ideas leading them to eventually set up their own experiments to answer a hypothesis. If, on the other hand, teachers ask the wrong type of question the children may think that there is a right or wrong answer in science and this may eventually close their minds to scientific investigations thus becoming apprehensive of failure.

- To develop teachers' confidence it is important to give them an outline of what children will do, once the correct question has been asked.
- Each activity is then linked to A.T.1 — not only to help teachers in record keeping but more importantly to help focus their attention on what the children are actually doing as opposed to what is assumed that the children are doing. The activities are linked to all the other relevant Science, English and Mathematics Attainment Targets for ease of recording hence assisting teachers to see cross curricular links.
- The teacher's Aids Sheets offer a reference for teachers to help them give ideas to children who find some aspects of the work difficult. These are not prescriptive as most children are extremely inventive in designing boats and aeroplanes etc. on their own.
- Worksheets provided for the children offer starting points relieving teachers from designing their own and they can therefore spend more time and energy working alongside the children.
- A list of resources is included to assist teachers in collecting equipment if science and technology is to be carried out more easily in the classroom.

Included in the pack are two story books which are ideal ways of starting a science investigation supported by Information Technology and a grid for recording the relevant Attainment Targets covered in this pack is provided. It is recommended that each topic is recorded on a sheet of acetate and used as overlays on the grid. This enables teachers to see at a glance the Statements of Attainments covered and those omitted. The pack also includes a pupils individual record sheets and a short list of useful book references.

As previously stated, the content of the children's work naturally fell into 3 areas — moving on land, water and through air. Moving on land starts with the idea that some objects move while others do not. The next activity involve moving balls in different ways. Friction is then investigated by the children and finally the shapes to make objects move easily are experimented with, leading to the use of rollers and wheels. Moving through water begins with playing with boats in the water tray and so developing familiarity with different hull shapes. Boat are then loaded to find out their stability. Children will then make boats out of junk and gradually add sails, steering and finally differing methods of propulsion to their boats. The problems of designing a safe slipway for their boats is then introduced. As the boats designs are developed the boats are then tested against each other and the idea of fair testing is introduced. Moving through air begins with the children trying to understand the concept that air is all around us even though we can not see it. To enable this to happen there are activities where air is moved either by fans, balloons or underwater. The difference between hot and cold air is the next concept to be investigated where the children are required to 'catch' the air. This naturally leads to the children developing parachutes. The idea of airflow is investigated and the children then make their own kites and aeroplanes. Once again these are tested to ascertain their effectiveness and their results recorded on the computer for interrogation. These activities were all tested and developed before inclusion in the curriculum file.

The final part of this pack are two computer programs **DISPLAY DATA** and **MOVEMENT TALES.**

Collecting data is fundamental to scientific investigation. The use of a computer to display and print it out neatly and accurately helps children to focus upon the interpretation of collected data. If children are allowed to use information technology themselves as part of their project work it follows that they are likely to develop much wider understanding of how to handle information.

A factor that teachers are very aware of in computer software is that many software packages require children to use language. However, working in schools where no child has English as his or her first language most computer programs designed for infants are unsuitable and not easily adaptable. As it was felt that it was unfair that children who could not necessarily read much English should be restricted in the use of the computer, a very popular computer program **RESOURCE's FAIRY TALES** was adapted for inclusion in the pack. Sixty sprites which are small graphic pictures were designed to go with the three moving themes. These sprites can be moved and placed on the screen to compose a picture on the theme of either on the road, at the beach, in the playground or at the airport. Text can be added by using concept keyboards or mouse if required to make an illustrated story, a description or poem, to be then printed out providing children with a tangible and rewarding result.

In conclusion, therefore, through using information technology to support activities in Science, young children are enabled to perform more complex investigations than previously accepted by traditional methods of teaching.

Further Reading:

MAPE [1989] *Primary Science: The Role of Information Technology.* Birmingham: Newman College.

Ritchie, R.[ed] [1988] *Using Computers to Support Primary Science and Technology.* Bristol: Avon LEA.

Ritchie, R. [1900] Science in the National Curriculum/ In Coulby, D. and Ward, S. *The Primary Core National Curriculum.* London: Cassell.

Chapter 12
Through the Looking Glass
Joyce I. Fields

This chapter will raise some of the issues which, in my opinion, will have a distinct influence upon the evolution and development of Information Technology usage in the primary curriculum over the next decade.

Primary Perspectives Dimension

Prior to the introduction to the National Curriculum of requirements in Information Technology, the use of the micro-computer throughout schools within the British state education system could justifiably have been described as 'haphazard'. Much depended upon the support and encouragement of the individual Local Education Authorities and their advisory teacher teams for the provision of hardware and software, as well as initial training programmes in the uses of micro-computers within the Primary classroom. Likewise, the key to success very much depended upon the enthusiasm and willingness of individual teachers to embrace the advent of a 'new age' revolution: the micro-chip explosion with its unchartered waters. It was a new adventure with no real indication as to its direction and eventual outcome.

Based upon the premise that the ways in which teachers utilise and use micro-computers effectively is a mirror image of their individual teaching experience and expertise, one of the principle primary perspectives is automatically enhanced *viz* the independent learner. Teachers providing a wide range of exciting stimulating learning environments naturally incorporate the use of current technological advances in their children's learning and the preparation of such children to take ownership for their own learning. Hence Information Technology capability can be defined as 'the conjunction of a facility to use Information Technology and an ability to use it appropriately, alongside other resources and methods, and to evaluate that use'. (Birnbaum, 1990).

In the Technology document Attainment Target 5 shows a progression in the tasks young children will be expected to experience and undertake, *viz* information handling—which starts long before they begin to work with micro-computers. The wide range of 'good sound primary practices', which they encounter can serve as the foundation for their understanding of micro-electronic forms of information storage, retrieval, interrogation and representation. It is important that children must be given structured opportunities to assist their understanding of the underlying organisation principles of databases and spreadsheets if they are to correctly access the information required.

In 1990 Underwood and Underwood's research has shown that there is a ranking in order of ease for the usage of information handling *viz* (a) lists, (b) hierarchies, (c) networks, and (d) tables. When their research subjects were given an accompanying skeletal diagram of the data structure it was found that 'list' and 'hierarchies' maintained their respective rank position, whilst 'tables' and 'networks' changed positions.

The implications for classroom practice being that pupils should encounter data structures in the named above order: list, hierarchies, tables, networks. The three most common data handling programs used in infant and junior schools are:

Program name	Data structure	Publisher
Lists	list	NCET
Sorting Game	hierarchy	NCET
First Facts	table	RESOURCE

It is essential that the children validate their data throughout collection and entry onto the micro-computer, otherwise conclusions may well be drawn which are erroneous through misconceptions and misunderstanding of the fundamental principles. It is imperative that young children are given a wide range of learning experiences to enhance prior concepts of traditional information storage and retrieval before being asked to use the micro-computer. Only then can children properly and appropriately take control of the new technology to assist them in their learning processes.

Children as young as three, four and five years are confident in their use of video records and are familiar with electronic supermarket check-outs, hence they can be described as having the bases for 'computer literacy'. Although such children do not have reading fluency, they do have a great deal of experience and expertise using electronically operated televisions, toys and video game suites. They are uninhibited and are free from the fears and suspicions held by many adults, so the teaching profession can no longer leave the Information Technology component of the National Curriculum to colleagues, who have specialism in this area.

There is a clear definite thrust forward by the school population who are acquiring a sound understanding of spreadsheets, databases and statistical inferences which were traditionally the preserve of a small elite adult world whose work in these specific areas required such instruments. Somekh and Davies (1991) argue for the need for teachers to become 'facilitators' ensuring progression and development of these skills and for young children to have more autonomy for their own learning by being active participants. Micro-computers can be justifiably build upon children's direct experience of their learning environment and can be utilised as a starting point or springboard for further investigations. For example, the immediacy of the response and accessibility of the 'Email' enables children to communicate rapidly thereby reinforcing enthusiasm and initial impetus of the learning. But there is in my opinion a cautionary note that although information retrieval and information handling can be a powerful 'tool' it is essential that the development of general information skills are not displaced by Information Technology skills.

Likewise, it must be remembered that one of the most important aspects of such a 'new technology revolution' is that the user must use available resources, be they traditional pen and paper or the micro-computer, in a relevant and realistic manner suitable to the task in hand.

European Dimension

One of the most important elements in 'crystal ball gazing' must be considerations related to the European dimension of education with the advent of 1992.

European education and inter-cultural education are important sources for heightening awareness of the nationalities and individual cultures throughout Europe as well as their positions within the framework of the European Economic Community [EEC].

Under the implementation of the National Curriculum in England, there is a legal requirement for multi-cultural education to be taught. Classrooms throughout England are becoming multi-cultural in consistency, as are classrooms further afield in Europe. Increasingly the interrelationships within such classrooms are becoming much more complex than they were twenty or thirty years ago. The norm for school populations during these years was that most schools traditionally had a static locally based catchment area. Now classroom are complex in structure as children from various backgrounds, cultures and countries make up their content.

> 'Classroom teachers are challenged by the concept that multi-cultural education deals with race, culture, language, social class, gender and handicap'.
>
> [Sleeter and Grant, 1988]

To this statement Tiedt and Tiedt [1989] suggest further factors, *viz*

> ' ... multi-cultural education is inter-disciplinary dealing with ... morality, attitudes and values.'

This raises the questions (a) how are present day teachers being supported and prepared to meet these increasing demands?, and (b) what are the effects of this in ter-cultural cross-fertilisation? There is a need for multi-cultural policies to be expanded to embrace this commonality of global experiences prevalent in the EEC. Throughout Europe classrooms are rapidly becoming multicultural *viz* Turkish im-migrants in Germany, Eastern European nationalities in France, Holland and Belgium, Romanians and Yugoslavians in Italy to name a few. There would appear, however, not to be a comprehensive policy to meet these needs, hence the complicated classroom structures which teachers are being asked to cope with have not yet been fully addressed.

I would suggest that one way of tackling such diverse problems is by harnessing the multi-media and information technological resources which have developed throughout Europe. With the use of the Interactive CD Rom, Electronic mail [Email] modem link systems and other micro-electronic advancements young children and their teachers are able to access information stored in databases created by their peers and/or for their peers, in other countries. This can be utilised effectively to expand their understanding and conceptualization of their locally based projects to broader issues of continental and global magnitude. Likewise, teachers will have the opportunity to exchange experiences and information using the same technologies.

Although physically the world has not shrunk, electronic communications have shrunk the world insofar as it is possible to receive news of world events almost immediately using interspace transmission. Thus, through the same information technology media educators and those involved in teaching and educational research, should be encouraged to exchange experiences and interact in a positive way, thereby developing each others understanding of the problems and 'positives' inherent in other European classrooms. By this sharing of expertise and experience each contributor will enhance his/her personal professional development and gain from the success and failures of others. Current technologies can very easily make this a reality without the added expense of substitute teachers, travelling expenses etc.

Through this interaction with other nationalities and cultures an understanding and appreciation of cultural differences could be nurtured in order that all children realise their inheritance as 'citizens of the world', thus wholeheartedly embracing the following statement:

> '[It] ...rejects the view that schools should seek to melt away cultural differences or the view that schools should merely tolerate cultural pluralism. Instead schools should be oriented towards the cultural enrichment of all children and youth through programs rooted to the preservation and extension of cultural alternatives.'

[AACTE, 1973 pages 264-265]

The National Centre for Educational Technology [NCET] conducted a survey in 1990, which demonstrated that although the above technologies are available few schools and educational establishments in England used or availed themselves of these facilities. This field is, therefore, obviously ripe for exploitation, expansion and harvesting within the primary perspectives in the National Curriculum.

Another avenue in which the issues raised by the shifting mobility in England and in Europe can be addressed is by introducing an inter-cultural element into the initial teacher training systems. Thereby trainee teachers as well as newly qualified teachers are in professional contact with their European counterparts through various technologies. This could be met by an enriching addition to the professional course syllabus for Initial Teacher training being European based as opposed to individual satellite states existing in isolation to one another as at the present time. This can be developed further with the interaction and use of technology as described above.

There is a real need to use this enormous resource. Perhaps this could be addressed if every teacher was given the opportunity to spend at least one term in more than one European country as a pre-requisite part of their professional training or up-dating courses, as well as teachers being given easily accessible communication with their European colleagues. This would heighten the participants awareness of the cultural differences, languages and socio-linguistic cultural factors in an informed manner.

I understand Britain is currently out of step with Europe as the thrust forward in Initial Teacher Education in Europe is moving further and further into University Institutes of Education and Colleges of Education bases for the academic and professional development of participants. At the present time, however, England's policy is increasingly passing the training of student teachers over to schools through a larger increase in the hours required to be spent on school experience practices as opposed to time spent in University or College of Education bases for professional development. Whilst there may be sound validity for such policies, again I would strongly advocate more communication and a sharing of experiences in order that all children are given equal opportunities for advancement and that all initial teacher training participants will have a sound, broad based understanding and appreciation of the versatility of information technology outside the obvious classroom learning situations.

Into the Future

The following might on first reading appear as a dream prediction, but it is not, in my opinion, any more advanced than the well-documented responses to the theory predictions voiced in the early 1980s. With the advent of the micro-chip, the micro-computer was an unfamiliar technology in unfamiliar, uncharted waters expected by many to burn itself out. Few would have or could have predicted the phenomenal speed or extent to which the micro-chip has since been developed and utilised permeating every aspect of life.

Like any structure which is embryonic the current history of information technology can be described as a scaffold which has had to be built to support the inner structure; to give foundations until the building can be formed and completed in its architectural design. I would suggest that the hardware and software acclaimed as a wonderful invention are now considered out of date yet their development was essential for the continuation of the phenomenally fast development of information technology.

On reflection some would argue that the design and selection of the scaffolding built to support the advancement of information technology was not the most appropriate. With the benefit of hindsight it is always easy to criticize and to make alternative recommendations. With all learning developments there has to be a period of inertia giving time to reflect and take stock; time to assess and evaluate; time to base valued judgements on the existing available evidence. The same line of development has not, however, been attributed to the rapid history of educational technologies. This rapid growth can be considered as a frontier of exploration. Yet in a short period of time it also will be surpassed as new frontiers are explored and new avenues are constructed without the essential period of reflection and re-evaluation. In my opinion, this could result in educationalists taking wrong decisions and wrong avenues for a sound progression of learning to be established.

Further, if the history of human existence is likened to a twelve hour clock face, the last quarter of an hour would represent the great advances, human discoveries and explorations the past one hundred years: the spurt of evolution. Human beings can be said to be a product of all the experiences which they have accumulated since their birth. Parallel to this is the development of the information technology clock face where the first quarter of an hour represents the spurt of evolution, which is the result of all technological experimentation and development to-date.

Today there is a new generation of micro-computers being developed for an eager market. The advent of the lap top micro-computers over the past two years, initially for executive business use, I feel confident will be recognized by parents, schools, and educators for its versatility and wide ranging application within the normal school learning environment and curriculum. Children will be able to commence a given curriculum project at school, down load onto disc, and then develop their ideas and work using their own lap top at home. Not only will basic information technology skills be reinforced but networks into the nationally stored data banks will be an easily accessible resource.

After reading the above the reader may raise the problem of using a keyboard with young children especially when there is no teacher assistance available. At the present time in the United States of America, there is an exciting experimental 'handpack' being developed. The 'handpack' is a handsize light and touch sensitive screen pad with a special stylus for writing on its surface. On this continuous loop system the user will be able to hand write details and information which the micro-computer 'handpack' will automatically decipher, and convert all 'typographical characters' and/or /graphic images' into publishers typescript before storing the given information. Thereby allowing for traditional methods of learning *viz* writing to continue, but in a very different media and dimension.

Voyager Software, Santa Monica, California, have developed some software packages which actually emulate the skill of 'reading a book'. All the information from the named book, for example 'The Snowman' is stored in a very small compact micro-chip where simulated 'page turning', 'quick flick through' and other normal facilities are available. Thereby allowing young children, as well as adults, the opportunity to use the synthesizer to 'read' or gain valuable relevant information. Also, there is a new innovation available which is the facility to annotate the users own notes into the margins of the 'book' exactly the same way as one can do with a printed form of a book. The ramifications of such a 'mind-blowing' innovation away from the traditional micro-computer is very exciting and far reaching.

What the eventual outcome of such convenient, versatile technological developments will be, only time will tell. There is no doubt that the best possible use of such advancements will be recognized, adapted and used by teachers in their pursuit of 'excellence in education' to meet the needs and challenges of children in the twenty-first century.

In conclusion, any prediction of the way in which the mushroom effect of information technology will develop can only be by speculation based on the evidence of evolution and development to-date. By gazing 'through the looking glass', however, it is reasonable to predict that there will be more contact between children of different nations using electronic advancement; teachers and educators will be in contact with each other for the betterment of morality, educational values and citizenship. Further advances in industry and the commercial world will have spin-off effects in schools. Children will gain an appreciation and comprehension of self motivation and self evaluation rather than being passive receivers of instruction. Thus tomorrow's children will be provided with opportunities to take ownership of their own learning and the main objective of present day educators will be realised: *the independent thinker* and *the independent learner*. Education as it is recognised, understand and known in this decade will be radically and intrinsically changed by the first two decades of the twenty-first century.

> 'Information technology will be the catalyst for radical change, and it will be the vehicle used for meeting the challenges ahead in the next century.'
>
> [Joyce I. Fields 1992]

Bibliography:

ACCTE Commission on 'Multi-cultural Education (1973). No One Model American'. *Journal of Teacher Education*, **24**, 264-265.

Birnbaum, I. (1990) *IT in the National Curriculum—Some Fundamental Issues*. RESOURCE.

Sleeter, C.E. and Grant, C.A. (1988) *Making Choices for Multi-cultural Education: Five Approaches to Race, Colour and Gender*. Columbus, OH: Charles E. Merrill.

Somekh, B. and Davies, R. (1991) Winning the Class Struggle. *Times Educational Supplement*, 23 August.

Tiedt, P.L. and Tiedt, I.M. (1986) *Multi-cultural Teaching: A Handbook of Activities, Information and Resources*. (2nd Ed.) Boston: Allyn and Bacon.

Underwood, J. and Underwood, G. (1990) *Computers and Learning*. Basil Blackwell.

APPENDIX A

Information Handling, Information Technology

throughout the National Curriculum

Statement of Attainment/Programme of study statements

Key Stage 1

Pupils should:

* locate information stored in a database; retrieve information and add to it: check the accuracy of entries.

Technology, AT5 POS

* use a word processor.

English, AT 3/4/5 POS

* refer to ......simple data on computers as a matter of course.

English, AT 2 POS

* enter and access information in a simple database.

Mathematics, AT 5

* be able to retrieve and select text, number, sound or graphics stored on a computer.

Science, AT 1

* be able to/use IT for the storage and retrieval of information.

Technology, AT 5

* be able to/use IT to make, amend and present information.

Technology, AT 5

* be able to collect information and enter it in a database ...and to select and retrieve information from the database.

Technology, AT 5

* be taught how to store, select and analyse information using software.

Technology, AT 5

* organise and present ideas using IT.

Technology, AT 5 POS

Key Stage 2

Pupils should:

* use IT to retrieve, develop, organise and present work.

Technology, AT 5

* amend and add to information an existing database, to check its plausibility and interrogate it.

Technology, AT 5

* use IT to present information in different forms for specific purposes.

Technology, AT 5

* use a software package to crease a computer database so that data can be captured, stored and retrieved.

Technology, AT 5

* insert and amend information in a computer database.

Technology, AT 5 POS

* find and present stored information.

Technology, AT 5 POS

* collect and organise information for entry into a database.

Technology, AT 5 POS

* use a data handling package to analyse and display [weather] information.

Geography, AT 8

* assemble ideas on paper or on a VDU.

English, AT 3

* have opportunities to create, polish and produce individually or together, by hand or on a word processor.

English, AT 3/4/5

* use spreadsheets or other computer facilities to explore number patterns.

Mathematics, AT 5

* interrogate data in a computer database.

Mathematics, AT 5

* insert and interrogate data in a computer database.

Mathematics, AT 5

* understand the uses of a range of devices for handling information and communication.

Science, AT 1

* use the computer to store, retrieve and present their work,

Science, POS

* have the opportunity to use and investigate the transmission and storage of information using computers

Science, POS

Key Stage 3

Pupils should:

* analyse and interpret data from complex secondary sources [for example, from a Census database].

Geography, AT 8

* have opportunities to produce writing and proof-read on a word processor.

English, AT 3/4/5 POS

* begin to use, with increasing confidence, information and data accessed from a computer.

Science, POS

* organise and express the results of historical study ...for example, by creating a database.

History, POS

* use IT to combine and organise different forms of information for a presentation to an audience.

Technology, AT 5

* select and interrogate a computer database to obtain information needed for a task.

Technology, AT 5

* know when it is appropriate to use a software package for a task rather than other means of information handling.

Technology, AT 5

Programme of study Statements

Pupils should be taught:

* to identify what should be done and ways in which work should be organised.

Technology, KS 1

* to organise their work, taking account of constraints.

Technology, KS 1

* to identify questions for enquiry, and plan and implement appropriate investigations.

Geography, KS 1-4

* to organise and plan their work carefully.

Technology, KS 2

* the raising and answering of questions.

Science, KS 2

APPENDIX B

Software Publishing Houses:

Useful Names and Addresses

4mation Educational Resources
Linden Lea
Rock Park
Barnstaple Devon
EX32 9AQ
Tel: 0271 45566

Acornsoft Ltd
Newmarket Road
Cambridge
CB2 EJN
Tel: 0223 3160390

Addison Wesley Ltd
Finchampstead Road
Wokingham
Berkshire
RG11 3NZ
Tel: 0734 794000

Advanced Memory Systems Ltd
166 Wilderspool Causeway
Warrington
WA4 6QA
Tel: 0925 413501

Advisory Unit
Endymion Road
Hatfield
Herts
AL10 8AU
Tel: 0727 65443

Ansa Sofware
Ansa UK Ltd
2 Bedford Square
London WC1 3RA
Tel: 01 631 798

Campbell Systems
7 Station Road
Epping
Essex CM16 4HA
Tel: 0373 77762

Arnold and Plant Ltd
31 Market Street
Whalley Bridge
Stockport
Cheshire

Ashton-Tate
1 Bath Road
Oaklands
Maidenhead SL6 4UH
Tel: 0628 33123

Aztec Software
25 St Mark Road
Deepcar
Sheffield
S30 5TF
Tel: 0742 862246

Beebug Ltd
Dolphin Place
Holywell Hill
St Albans Herts
Tel: 0727 40303

BP Educational Services
PO Box 5
Wetherby
West Yorkshire
LS23 6YY
Tel: 0937 843477

Cambridge Micro Software
The Edinburg Building
Shaftesbury Road
Cambridge CB2 2RU
Tel: 0223 312393

Colin Rowlinson Software
2 Tamar Road
Haydock
St Helens WA11 0HR

Camsoft
Unit 2
Maen Offeren
Blaenau Ffestiniog
Tel: 0766 831878

Caxton Software Ltd
10-14 Bedford Square
Covent Garden
London
WC2E 9HE
Tel: 01 379 6502

Chalksoft Ltd
PO Box 49
Spalding
Lincs PE11 1NZ
Tel: 0775 69518

Clares Micro Supplies
98 Middlewich Road
Rudheath
Northwich Cheshire
CW9 7DA
Tel: 0606 48511

COIC
Sales Department
Moorfoot
Sheffield
S1 4PQ
Tel: 0742 704563

Duncan Databases
9 Chestnut Grove
New Malden
Surrey KT3 3JS
Tel: 01 942 2538

ESM
Duke Street
Wisbech
Cambridgeshire
PE13 2AE
Tel: 0945 63441

Grafox
South Bank Technopark
90 London Road
London
SE1 6JN
Tel: 01 922 8807

Communitel Ltd
189 Firston Road
London
W10 6TH
Tel: 01 960 7998

Compsoft plc
Compsoft Manor
Farncombe Hill
Godalming Surrey
GU7 2AR
Tel: 04868 25925

Computer Concepts Ltd
Gaddesden Place
Hemel Hempstead
Herts HP2 6EX
Tel: 0442 63933

Cornix Software
Spirella Building
Letchworth
Herts
SG6 4ET
Tel: 0462 682989

Database Publications
Europa House
68 Chester Road
Hazel Grove
Stockport SK7 5NY
Tel: 061 456 8383

ILECC
John Rushkin Street
London
SE5 0PQ
Tel: 01 735 9123

ITVA Ltd
6 Paul Street
London
EC2A 4JH
Tel: 01 247 5206

Limrose Software
Aerial Road
Llay Industrial Estate
Wrexham Clwyd
LL12 0TU
Tel: 097 883 5555

GSN Educational Software
214 Stamford Street
Ashton under Lyne
Lancs OL6 7LP
Tel: 061 339 6635

Head Computers Ltd
Oxted Mill
Spring Lane
Oxted
Surrey RH8 9PB
Tel: 0883 717057

Holmfirth Academy
32 Boscastle Close
Yatton
Avon
Tel: 0284 687750

Management Data Systems Ltd
108 Parthenon Drive
Liverpool
L11 7AQ
Tel: 051 226 1214

MAPE
76 Sudbrooke Holme Drive
Sudbrooke
Lincs LN2 2SF
Tel: 0522 754408

Mertec Computer Products
35/36 Singleton Street
Swansea
SA1 3QN
Tel: 0792 467980

MESU
Sir William Lyons Road
University of Warwick
Conventry
CV4 7EZ
Tel: 0203 416994

Micro Express Ltd
Studland Road
Kingsthorpe
Northampton NN2 6NA
Tel: 0604 791010

Logotron Ltd
Dales Brewery
Gwydir Street
Cambridge CB1 2LJ
Tel: 0223 323656

Longman Micro Software
Longman House
Burnt Hill
Harlow
Essex CM20 2JE
Tel: 0279 26721

Lotus Development UK Ltd
Consort House
Victoria Street
Windsor, Berks SL4 1EX
Tel: 0753 840281

Minerva Systems
69 Sidwell Street
Exeter
Devon EX4 6PH
Tel: 0392 37756

MUSE
PO Box 43
Houghton on the Hill
Leicester LE7 9GX
Tel: 0533 433839

NEOW Software
Unit 12, Progress Business Centre
Whittle Parkway
Slough SL1 6DQ
Tel: 06286 68334

Nerick Automation Ltd
Gunsell Lodge
Wood Lane
Tugby
Leicester

Newman College
Bartley Green
Birmingham
B32 3NT
Tel: 021 476 1181

Microbel
The Loft
Lord Nelson Yard
Sutton on Trent
Newark, Notts NG23 6PF
Tel: 0636 821722

Norwich Computer Services
18 Mile End Road
Norwich
Norfolk
NR4 7QY
Tel: 0603 507057

PFS Software/EDHITEC
7 Carlton Road
Harrogate
North Yorks
HG2 8DD
Tel: 0423 871027

Precision Software Ltd
6 Park Terrace
Worcester Park
Surrey
KT4 7JZ
Tel: 01 330 7166

Psion Software Ltd
Harcourt Street
London
W1H 1DT
Tel: 01 723 9408

Pyramid Computer Systems Ltd
9 Church Street
Reading
Berks
Tel: 0734 595633

Research Machines Ltd
PO Box 75
Mill Street
Oxford
OX2 0BW
Tel: 0865 249886

Somerset Info. Tech. Unit
SCAT
Wellington Road
Taunton, Somerset TA1 5AX
Tel: 0823 289411

Newstar Software
200 North Service Rd
Brentwood
Essex
CM14 4SG
Tel: 0277 220573

Resource
Exeter Road
Off Coventry Grove
Doncaster
DN2 2PY
Tel: 0302 63800/63784

Sagesoft plc
NEI House
Regent Centre
Newcastle upon Tyne
NE3 3DS
Tel: 091 284 7077

Sapphire Systems Ltd
Wellesley House
102 Cranbrook Road
Ilford Essex
IG1 4NH
Tel: 01 554 0582

Satchel Software
Haydon House
Alcester Road
Studley, Warks
Tel: 0386 792617

School Fax
24 Somerset Road
Swindon
Wiltshire
SN2 1NF

Sentinel Software
Wordperfect UK
Wellington House
New Zealand Avenue
Walton on Thames KT12 1PY
Tel: 0932 231164

Watford Electronics
250 Lower High St
Watford
Herts WD1 2AN
Tel: 0923 37774

Southdata Ltd
Voysey House
Barley Mow Passage
London
W4 4PT
Tel: 01 995 7587/7967

SPA
Software Production Associates
PO Box 59
Leamington Spa CV31 3QA
Tel: 0926 22959

Suffolk Educational Software
c/o B. Massey
County Hall
Ipswich
Suffolk
Tel: 0473 55801

Tecmedia Ltd
5 Granby Street
Loughborough
Leicestershire LE11 3DU
Tel: 0509 230248

Trafford Computing
7 Trafford Road
Alderley Edge
Cheshire SK9 7NT
Tel: 0625 583686

Whittle Systems
53 Besselsleigh Rd
Wooton
Abingdon Oxford
OX13 6DX
Tel: 0865 736488

APPENDIX C

Notes on Contributors

Derek Allen, Headteacher, Snaith County Primary School, Snaith, nr Goole, Humberside, UK

Peter Avis, Director of NCET, Sir William Lyons Road, University of Warwick Science Park, Coventry CV4 7EZ, UK

Michael A. Bortoft, Lecturer in Information Technology, University College, Scarborough, UK

Rod Buckle, Deputy Headteacher, Springhead Special School, Scarborough, UK

Alison Drage, Teacher, Southall First and Middle School, Southall, London, UK

Joyce I. Fields, Institute of Education, University of Hull, Cottingham Road, Hull HU6 7RX, UK

Kathleen Guthrie, HUMMEC, The Teachers Centre, Coronation Road, Hull, UK

Stephen Heppell, Department of Education, Anglia Higher Education, HUMMEC, The Teachers Centre, Coronation Road, Hull, UK

David F. Sewell, Psychology Department, University of Hull, Cottingham Road, Hull HU6 7RX, UK

Michael H. Wright, Senior Adviser SEN, Humberside LEA, Prospect House, Prospect Street, Hull, UK

INDEX